MW00612333

GOALTENDERS

are not

TARGETS

Becoming an ELITE GOALTENDER

Written for

COACHES and EDUCATED GOALTENDERS
OF ALL AGES
including the <u>Pros</u>!

by

Brent Bradford
&
Vic LeMire

Copyright © 2011, Brent Bradford Enterprises Ltd.
& Vic LeMire

®Bradford's Goal Academy & Design is a
Registered Trademark of
Brent Bradford Enterprises Ltd.

Cover and Interior Photos by:
Brent Bradford & Vic LeMire

Printed in Taiwan by
RED & BLUE COLOR PRINTING CO., LTD.
New Taipei City, Taiwan

ISBN 9781-89264-000-0
UPC 0-30955-03963-3

Edited and Published by:

Brent Bradford
brent@bradfordsgoalacademy.com

Vic LeMire
vics@netzero.com

No part of this publication may be reproduced, stored in a retrieval system or transmitted, photocopied or any other reprographic copying in any form or by any means without the prior permission of the publisher.

DEDICATION - *BRENT BRADFORD*

This book is dedicated to my Grandparents: Clifton and Margaret (Mailey) Bradford & George and Mary (Wickenheiser) Pettigrew. Thank you very much for your unconditional support toward the development of my athletic and academic skills throughout my life! You answered the call without hesitation whenever something was needed (e.g., meals, rides, supportive talks, and much, much more)! I consider myself lucky to have such amazing Grandparents!

I would also like to dedicate this book to all the goaltenders that I have been fortunate enough to have coached and mentored over the past twenty-two years. It is because of you that I keep putting my skates and goal pads on each week to run Bradford's Goal Academy!

Visit Bradford's Goal Academy at
www.bbga.ca

ABOUT THE AUTHOR - *BRENT BRADFORD*

Brent Bradford, Academy Dean and Founder of Bradford's Goal Academy, began training goaltenders at fifteen years old. Following a hockey career that brought the fortune of being part of two National-winning hockey teams, *Kelowna Spartans - 1993 Jr. A Centennial Cup (now - Royal Bank Cup)* and *University of Alberta Golden Bears - 1999 CIAU University Cup*, Brent went on to earn a high level of education at the University of Alberta (i.e., Bachelor of Education Degree, Specialization Diploma in Education, Master of Education Degree).

During a ten-year teaching career in Elementary and Junior High School, Brent was recognized as an award-winning educator, resource developer, program innovator, district liaison, and leader in the area of Physical Education. He recently returned to the University of Alberta to pursue a Doctor of Philosophy Degree. In 2011, Brent was recognized as an award-winning Teacher Educator at the University of Alberta (teaching pre-service school teachers).

Brent - Trail, BC Atom Rep - 1982   *Centennial Cup with Brent & his Father - 1993*

Brent has taught goaltenders of all ages and hockey levels. He continues to develop his clientele both on and off the ice and in the classroom. Bradford's Goal Academy stresses the importance of a solid education. He rewards his goaltenders when they attain high grades in school. Brent is involved in Global Sports Scouting Services Inc. assisting in the recruitment of top-calibre athletes. Brent's education and passion towards healthy, active living and decreasing the high number of sedentary lifestyles urged him to create his second business, called FITIVITY ᴛᴍ Ltd. (www.fitivity.com).

DEDICATION - *VIC LeMIRE*

Goaltenders are not Targets - Revised Edition, in all its editorial grandeur, brings together such incredible memories of life-long hockey friends, and colleagues. An accumulation of 32 years of coaching, mentoring, and training hockey goaltenders and players has laid the special framework of the book's educational content!

Acknowledging close friends, such as co-author Brent Bradford - Roy, Jan, Bobby, and Taylor Henderson of Global Sports Scouting Services Inc. - Jas, Liam, Charlie, and Myra Qualitz - Dave Wood, who is my Brother in CHRIST, and all my first class Instructors of Vic's Hockey Schools & Equipment Ltd. (each contributed wholeheartedly, his/her very special part in my life), can demonstrate merely a fraction of my devotion toward them all!

It is with my deepest love that I dedicate this book to my Mom - Cecile LeMire, who's forever, unselfish love gave me the home life others only wish they had. And to my Father - Vic LeMire Sr. - World Champion Professional Wrestler, who provided me with life's wisdom and competitive dedication I would require to become the Grand Master of Goaltending Instruction throughout the Hockey World!

Love You Mom   **Love You Dad**

ABOUT THE AUTHOR - *VIC LeMIRE*

Vic LeMire, Founder, President, and CEO of Vic's Hockey Schools & Equipment Ltd. (1973 - present) created ground breaking methods of goaltender instruction through his many specialized classes in Canada, USA, and Japan.

Vic, who is recognized as a best-selling author of two goaltending books - *Goaltenders are not Targets* (1998) (*aka The Goaltender's Bible by USA Olympic Hockey Team Goaltender in an article - USA Today*) and *Off the Post* (1999) (*written for Advanced Level Goaltenders and Coaches*), has the following credentials behind him: *Coach/Graduate - Level 3 CAHA/USA Coaches Certification Program, Instructor/Coach - Canadian Junior Olympic Program, Educated in Mechanical Engineering (while attending Ohio University, Denver University, and UBC on full Hockey Scholarships)*. Vic has also assisted with *Global Sports Scouting Services*.

"Great Save"
A
Save to
Remember !

Vic's coaching career and credentials include Canadian Major Junior - New Westminster Bruins, BCHL Junior "A" - Langley Thunder, Kelowna Spartans, and Surrey Eagles. Vic has coached numerous Professional, University, College, and Junior hockey goaltenders and players. A few professional players he has coached include: Olaf Kolzig, goaltender 14 NHL seasons; Stu Barnes, 19 NHL seasons; Allan Bester, 11 NHL seasons; Mark Fitzpatrick, 10 NHL seasons; Jayson More, 10 NHL seasons; Ian Clark, 11 NHL seasons (Goaltender Consultant).

GENUINE HISTORY

Brent Bradford & **Vic LeMire** have joined forces to write one of the most exceptional pieces of literature available concerning the goaltending position. The rich amount of history between Brent & Vic has helped develop the latest volume of ***Goaltenders are not Targets*** which is based on:

1. Research
2. Personal Experience
3. Background Knowledge

Combing the minds of both Brent and Vic has helped develop an excellent resource for anyone interested in learning more about the Art of Goaltending!
/ Bantam AAA Goaltender Parent

Above: (1991) Vic and Brent after an intense workout prior to a Junior 'A' Training Camp
Below: (1990) Brent instructing at Vic's Hockey Schools
Below: (1983) Brent learning to be an effective skater at Vic's Hockey Schools

TABLE OF CONTENTS

INTRODUCTION

Goaltenders are not Targets has been written for goaltenders of all ages, parents/guardians, coaches, and anyone else who wishes to delve into the ***art of goaltending***. The major objective for this book is to respond productively to the many common questions below. We face these questions regularly each time we enter a hockey environment.

Goaltenders state...

As I head into a new hockey season...

1. Are there any reference materials to assist me throughout the hockey season when I may be struggling with a goaltending concept?

2. How can I relay the information I have learned about goaltending to my coaches during the hockey season?

3. Is there any reading material specific to goaltending available that I can read on a regular basis in order to keep up with my goaltending, reading, and comprehension skills?

Parents/Guardians state...

I know very little about the goaltending position...

1. Are there any written materials that may be used as a reference tool throughout the hockey season that supports what my goaltender has learned thus far?

2. How can I assist my goaltender throughout the hockey season?

3. What type of equipment should I purchase for my goaltender and what makes one set of goaltender equipment different from another?

4. What size of goal pads should my goaltender wear?

5. When do you recommend I purchase goal skates for my goaltender?

6. How do I know the size of the stick that my child should use when playing goal?

Coaches state...

My background knowledge about the goaltending position is minimal...

1. What are some coaching strategies I can use with my goaltenders during practices to support their skill development?

2. How much of the position is mechanical, physical, and/or mental?

3. How do I know if my goaltender's equipment is too small, big, etc...?

4. How can my goaltender help strengthen the team's game plan besides stopping the puck?

ATTENTION: This book has been specifically designed to respond to these questions and many others that are raised in hockey environments across the world concerning goaltenders. It covers a wide range of topic areas (e.g., skill development, equipment information, positioning tactics, practice drills, game strategies, mental training components, and much, much more).

It is important to note what works well for one goaltender may not work as well for another. This book outlines the key concepts surrounding the *art of goaltending*; it will stimulate ideas and assist the goaltender in becoming more confident while developing into a more valuable part of the team.

Quick tips surrounding the topic area of conditioning will be focused upon throughout the book. Pre- and post-season conditioning is of critical importance for goaltenders. Parents/guardians and coaches can play an integral part in enhancing a goaltender's level of conditioning. The conditioning tips are outlined so that the goaltender is better equipped to initiate a self-development program while maintaining a high level of enjoyment and challenges.

This book is intended to be a reference tool, which can help establish a positive understanding and a strong relationship between goaltenders, teammates, parents/guardians, and coaches. It is purposefully dedicated to strengthen this relationship so that goaltenders will be able to face each game, practice, and shot with positive frames of mind and efficient levels of anticipation. Goaltenders are extremely critical to their team's level of success. They are the *last line of defence* and are called on to stop an opposing team's rush and make that *great save* on a consistent basis.

When was the last time you saw a goaltender make that
GREAT GAME-WINNING SAVE?

GR8 Save!

GREAT GAME-WINNING SAVES …
ARE ALWAYS REMEMBERED BY GOALTENDERS!

PART ONE

PHILOSOPHY OF GOALTENDING

CHAPTER 1 - WHAT IS GOALTENTDING?

Goaltending in the Game of Hockey remains one of the most exciting and demanding positions in any sport. A goaltender's performance has a lasting effect on the team's level of success. A coach does not have the luxury of hiding a goaltender on the ice as can be done with other positional players at various times during a game. A goaltender must be well prepared at all times and has endless opportunities to make great saves and to assist in the team's game plan from the backside.

Goaltending is psychologically demanding. Goaltenders must be able to control the environment; the environment must not control the goaltenders. They are required to be focused on the puck at all times prepared to react to every shot while communicating to teammates about incoming offensive attacks. They must be aggressive in order to show the puck as little of the net as possible while still being attentive to angles and positioning.

More advanced goaltenders must possess the ability to anticipate before having to make a save. It is important for these goaltenders to decipher a play in progress and to conclude what will happen to the puck after a save. Goaltenders need to become *Great Chess Masters* in the Game of Hockey!

Who would ever want to be a goaltender? A goaltender can be anyone willing to put on goaltender equipment and stand in the goal crease while players fire pucks toward the net.

However, a ***GREAT*** goaltender is made up of a person who:

- takes pleasure in facing a challenge and communicates effectively
- wishes to make a difference in a game and is mentally tough
- understands the importance of focussing
- enjoys working hard at skill-building
- enjoys all the rewards from parents/guardians, coaches, and fans after a **GREAT GAME**
- strives to understand offensive strategies (e.g., 2-1-2)

The goaltending position is unique. Although challenging, it is a position that demands holistically a high level of conditioning. It has been said that ***goaltending*** *is played 80-90%* ***mentally*** *and 10-20%* ***physically***.

ATTENTION: Being in charge of stopping pucks for a team will bring on bruises, pressure, and criticism. A goaltender that develops the fundamentals and continues to enhance necessary skills will soon find out that it is one of the most enjoyable positions to engage in. A goaltender that continues to increase his/her level of strength and conditioning will progress to higher levels of hockey more easily. A goaltender that wears proper fitting equipment will remain safe while striving to stop pucks from all angles.

The equipment today is well-built. It offers the puck minimal amounts of area to injure a goaltender (if the goaltender wears it properly and does not shy away from the puck). Of course the goaltender may get a few bruises here and there throughout the season; proper fitting equipment will minimize the extreme cases.

Goaltending has changed over the years! If you watch goaltenders from different hockey eras, you will realize quickly that much has been transformed (e.g., equipment, crease lines). It is important to note that ***there is no ONE WAY*** to play the goaltending position.

Each goaltender will bring different characteristics to a hockey team (e.g., size, speed, agility, puck-handling skills, confidence, experience, etc.).

Therefore, each goaltender will develop a ***personal goaltender system***, or overall approach to keep the puck from entering the net. Whatever style the goaltender chooses to engage in, it remains critical that he/she strives to enhance his/her skills by observing others, experimenting with new skill sets, inquiring about new information, and practising at every opportunity.

Goaltenders must be students of the game! Goaltenders MUST be challenged by coaches and parents/guardians. Their knowledge must be tested consistently (e.g., the knowledge of responsibilities of not only their own position, but those of teammates and the other team). Goaltenders who **study the game of hockey** will recognize plays, strategies, and offensive attacks before they even occur. They will begin to think ahead of the play (**Chess Masters of the Game**); they will not react after the play has occurred and after the puck has gone past forcing the RED LIGHT to be turned on. Goaltenders must develop a **high level of overall hockey knowledge**. They must understand the Game of Hockey to a higher degree than solely knowing how to stop a puck.

QUESTION: Have you ever wondered why so many coaches and the vast majority of colour play-by-play analysts on all the major television networks are former professional goaltenders?

Coaching goaltenders is not an easy task! Whether a coach or parent/guardian has been a goaltender previously or not, it is important to recognize that goaltending has changed.

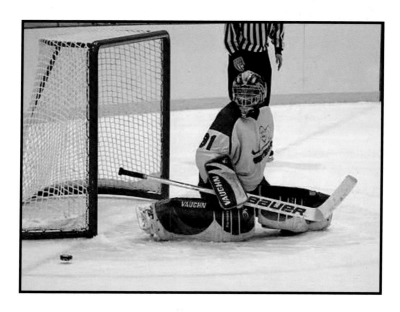

Today's goaltenders require a special way of being coached. Although the techniques and skills are straightforward, logical, and easy to learn, coaching goaltenders requires a positive, constructive, and innovative learning environment; goaltenders of all levels learn most effectively in an environment where they are taught properly with a caring attitude, not one that attacks the goaltender's efforts and skills, and not one that relegates the goaltenders into becoming nothing more than a *TARGET!* Although it is the most demanding position, goaltending must remain fun!

Goaltenders must be one of the best skaters on the team! Traditionally, and usually in lower levels of hockey, goaltenders have been identified for their lack of skating abilities, lack of hockey sense, and/or quiet demeanour in the dressing room.

Goaltenders have often been called *TARGETS* until they develop the skills and knowledge surrounding advanced strategies in order to challenge and defeat any hockey player who dares to score a goal! Then, and only then, can a goaltender state, *"I belong to the elite fraternity of goaltending!"*

ATTENTION GOALTENDERS: You have made a conscious decision to play a position that will enable you to be a difference-maker. Take every opportunity to study the Game of Hockey and to practice your individual skills so that you can be the most effective goaltender in your league.

Go Make A Difference!

As you continue to read *Goaltenders are not Targets*, we strongly suggest that you:

✓ make notes within each chapter
✓ refer back to specific chapters during the hockey season
✓ share with your parents/guardians/coaches any new information that you believe will help you and your team make educated hockey decisions

The pressures are tremendous …
the rewards are even greater!

Goaltending is the greatest position to play in hockey! Now continue reading *Goaltenders are not Targets* and become primed to have a winning season and a stellar career!

Did You Know …

Kelly Hrudey was the winning goaltender for the New York Islanders during the "Easter Epic" (i.e., a four-overtime Game 7 thriller in 1987). Hrudey went on to be known as "Hollywood" when he played goal for the Los Angeles Kings.

CHAPTER 2 - GOALTENDER EQUIPMENT

A goaltender's equipment holds as much, if not more, importance than the skills he/she is developing. It is essential that goaltender equipment matches the level of play and the age of goaltenders wearing it. There are three key topic areas that need to be addressed when purchasing goaltender equipment; they are **protection, mobility,** and **cost.**

Protection: If a goaltender is not well protected, he/she will not play the position for an extended period of time due to numerous injuries. Protection is the most important reason for choosing proper goaltender equipment. If equipment that is purchased is too small or worn out, a goaltender will not receive the required protection. Good used equipment can be repaired. Consideration should be given to purchasing goaltender pads, blockers, trappers, etc. which can be repaired and are the correct size. If the equipment protects the proper areas, it is worth wearing (no matter what the color or brand name).

Mobility: A goaltender must be able to move effortlessly in and around the crease area. If the equipment is blocking any required movements, adjustments MUST be made. Choosing to wear trappers, blockers, goaltender pads, etc. which are too big is NOT an effective strategy for a goaltender; the equipment will be too heavy and too bulky.

Cost: The cost of goaltender equipment on average is exceedingly higher than that of forwards or defensemen; however, we strongly believe that proper fitting, well-protective goaltender equipment does not always require the family's credit card to be present. Good used equipment that has been properly cared for can be just as effective as brand new products.

ATTENTION: On the flip side, a goaltender that takes extra care of his/her equipment will reap physical and financial rewards. Physically, equipment will last longer and will work as it should during games (e.g., not broken down, not ripped, not missing important straps). Financially, when it becomes too small and reaches a point of **no more self-adjustments,** equipment can be traded or sold for a decent, fair price if it is in good-quality working condition. If goaltender equipment is not cared for properly, it will not work as it should during games and will usually be worth very little when it is outgrown. We trust this point is understood; proper care of goaltender equipment can be beneficial both physically and financially!

Self-Adjustment Tips: Throughout a hockey season, a goaltender will almost certainly grow in height, weight, and/or strength. This does not mean that a goaltender must go back to the sports store and purchase new equipment that fits meticulously. It is important to become acquainted with the way goaltender equipment is assembled so adjustments, add-ons, and improvements can be made by the goaltender him/herself. This will allow for the equipment to keep offering the proper amount of protection and mobility as the goaltender develops gradually in height, weight, and/or strength.

NOTE TO GOALTENDERS: To be a GREAT goaltender, protection and mobility is absolutely essential! It is *good practice* to check your equipment for protection and mobility purposes a few times during the hockey season with a family member; the family member can act as the observer and look for areas that may not be protecting the body and for areas of immobility. This can be another great opportunity to spend some quality family/goaltender time in the confines of the family home!

NOTE TO PARENTS/GUARDIANS: Goaltenders, especially young and inexperienced ones, DO NOT require the top of the line equipment to perform effectively; the equipment needs to meet three requirements that will impact either the goaltender and/or the family (i.e., protection, mobility, and cost). Purchasing equipment that has been broken in by older and larger goaltenders that have outgrown it is an effective strategy that can usually meet these three requirements. Throughout this chapter, strategies will be discussed in order to enhance used goaltender equipment (e.g., adding or modifying specific pieces of equipment will save on bruises and money)!

COMMON QUESTION: What is the best trapper, blocker, goaltender pads, etc. on the market? We have yet to come across a specific brand name that serves the purposes of all goaltenders. It is important to note that each goaltender is different (e.g., size, speed, strength), so different types of goaltender equipment will need to be searched out on an individual basis. However, when choosing proper fitting equipment, there are some considerations that must be addressed. These considerations will be discussed in specific sections throughout this chapter.

Coach Brent Bradford and Coach Vic LeMire
present the
GOALTENDER EQUIPMENT CHECKLIST

Goaltender equipment must:

1. be comfortable
2. be protective in all areas
3. be affordable
4. be well taken care of
5. enable a high level of mobility

To be a confident goaltender, one who does not shy away from the puck and one who enjoys reacting to every play that arises (e.g., playing the puck), the equipment must be in good-quality working condition throughout the hockey season!

UNDERWEAR. Goaltenders MUST make practical decisions about what will be worn underneath their equipment. They must be attentive to the following list when choosing what to wear as UNDERWEAR. UNDERWEAR must provide comfort, mobility, warmth, and protection.

Underwear MUST be comfortable for goaltenders. If goaltenders spend their time uncomfortable on the ice due to itchy clothes, unwanted sweat dripping down the back, rashes being exposed, etc., their attention will most certainly not be on stopping pucks. Today, as opposed to years ago, there are many new brands of UNDERWEAR that have been developed to assist goaltenders in remaining comfortable on the ice while maintaining the necessity of mobility, warmth, and protection (e.g., light-weight, perspiration-controlling, and protective material). Long-sleeve shirts, long pants, and tube socks are the minimum requirements for goaltenders. Turtle-neck shirts (with protective material, e.g., Kevlar) are recommended for warmth and added protection from possible skate cuts. Tube socks are highly recommended!

GAME SITUATION TO AVOID: When a goaltender goes into the butterfly position, a player may cut across the crease behind him/her after a play and may possibly step on the goaltender's Achilles Tendon. **This has been observed before!** Tube socks and long pants can play a vital role in protecting this area in an extreme situation such as this. We observe, on a consistent basis, goaltenders not wearing proper tube socks which extend past the Achilles Tendon. It is frightening to wonder what would happen if a player accidentally stepped on that body part!

ATTENTION GOALTENDERS: DO NOT step onto the ice without UNDERWEAR on the upper body, legs, and feet. Goaltenders that choose to do this are simply asking for cuts and scrapes (e.g., from goal pad straps), rashes (e.g., from velcro and other materials sliding back and forth on the skin) and potential year-ending injuries (e.g., skate cuts). UNDERWEAR that is light-weight, keeps you warm enough (especially in cold arenas and/or when the play is in the other end), controls perspiration, and covers and protects exposed body parts are important considerations.

Coach Brent Bradford and Coach Vic LeMire state:
IT IS NOT A FASHION SHOW ON THE ICE...
STAY COMFORTABLE, MOBILE, WARM, AND PROTECTED!

PROTECTIVE CUP/ATHLETIC SUPPORT. Goaltenders DO NOT wear the same athletic support as forwards and defensemen. Goaltenders MUST wear a specialized PROTECTIVE CUP in order to maintain a high level of protection from direct and indirect shots and nearby hockey sticks which are *digging* for loose pucks. They must also stay protected when they fall onto their backsides; in this situation, the puck could possibly be shot and strike the goaltender between the legs (a player's cup will NOT protect a goaltender in this situation). It is important to note that a major difference between a player's cup and a goaltender's PROTECTIVE CUP, besides the added protection above and to the sides of the main area (e.g., pelvic area), is that a PROTECTIVE CUP is *banana-shaped* to protect goaltenders that fall onto their backsides and expose important body parts.

PROTECTIVE CUPS come in all sizes (e.g., Junior, Intermediate, and Senior). They have been enhanced, over the years, to fit the waist and the body suitably. It is imperative that goaltenders wear a proper fitting PROTECTIVE CUP (e.g., no looseness or movement) which provides a sufficient amount of protection. If a goaltender purchases a **PROTECTIVE CUP** that is too small, it will NOT provide the amount of protection that is required. On the contrary, if a goaltender purchases a PROTECTIVE CUP that is too big, it will move around and will dig into the stomach area, which can inhibit the level of mobility.

Tip #1 - The straps on the PROTECTIVE CUP should be replaced when they become worn out, stretched, and/or weak. If a goaltender's PROTECTIVE CUP does not fit properly, serious injuries can occur. This IMPORTANT piece of equipment is NOT expensive; goaltenders MUST NOT step onto the ice without wearing a PROTECTIVE CUP that fits properly!

FEMALE GOALTENDERS: It is highly recommended that ALL female goaltenders wear a properly fitting Goaltender Jock Jill (See Tip #1 above).

GOAL STICK. *Is my Goaltender's Stick the Correct Size?* As a tool for success, the *Goal Stick* is one of the goaltender's most important pieces of equipment. Knowing the correct size and many other important features of the *Goal Stick* that each goaltender must consider, leaves a hockey parent with many questions of what to do!

ATTENTION PARENTS AND GOALTENDERS: You MUST understand that the new modern day material used in manufacturing *Senior-Sized Goal Sticks* produces very light-weight sticks.

A goaltender should attempt to use the biggest, longest *Goal Stick* he/she could physically handle with ease. This suggestion may involve the goaltender to start with a senior model stick and "cut" it down to a manageable size considering the goaltender's age, height, and strength.

What Size? When a goaltender is deciding on the size of his/her goal stick, there are important considerations that must be adhered to. These considerations include the following:

- When the goaltender is in his/her Ready (SET) Position, with the blade of the Goal Stick flat on the ice, an observer using a front view of the goaltender MUST take notice of two possible problems that may become visible. An incorrect Blocker positioning may be created if a *Goal Stick* is the wrong size. Consider the two possible problems listed below:
    - o if there is a hole between the goaltender's arm and his/her body (the stick is too long)
    - o if the Blocker covers part of the goaltender's leg pad (the stick is too short)
- There must not be any space between the goaltender's elbow and his/her waist and the Blocker must not cover any part of the leg pad

ATTENTION PARENTS AND GOALTENDERS: Once you see the Blocker positioning, you can now determine if the goaltender needs to hold the *Goal Stick* higher or lower on the shaft to eliminate the problems listed above.

The Formula To Use In Cutting A Goal Stick Down To Size Is As Follows:

If you need to cut the wide, barrel portion of the *Goal Stick*, you MUST also cut an equal length off of the top end of the shaft (i.e., when the wide, barrel portion of the *Goal Stick* is shortened by one inch, then an equal one inch length must be cut off of the top end of the shaft to promote a continued balanced weight distribution in the *Goal Stick*).

ATTENTION PARENTS AND GOALTENDERS: When you are cutting into the wide barrel portion of the newly designed, modern day *Goal Stick*, you will discover that an open, hollow barrel becomes exposed. You MUST finish the customization of this *Goal Stick* by preparing a small fiberglass repair to cover the open barrel.

HINT: Most hardware stores supply simple fiberglass repair kits to perform this minor customization of the *Goal Stick*. Once it is dried (cured), a little light sanding over the fiberglass repair and some paint will complete the job nicely. This customization procedure of the *Goal Stick* provides the goaltender with a very strong, well-balanced, and properly sized *Goal Stick* to use effectively.

GOAL SKATES versus PLAYER SKATES. Once an individual decides to become a full-time goaltender, he/she should begin to wear Goal Skates. Goaltenders are required to perform a variety of skating skills in order to meet the demands of stopping pucks. There are several differences and advantages between Goal Skates and Player Skates.

1. Blades - Goal Skates have wider blades and are intended to have more blade on the ice at all times. This long, flat blade produces a strong, solid stance on the ice. Goal Skates are sharpened differently than Player Skates in order to allow goaltenders to have more of a straight blade on the ice which helps with balance and mobility as opposed to Player Skates.

2. Protection - Goal Skates are built with more protection than Player Skates in order to keep goaltenders from becoming injured when stopping pucks.

3. Mobility - Goal Skates allow goaltenders to have more mobility when performing goaltender specific-skating skills than Player Skates can allow. Goal Skates keep the goaltender solid on the ice while making the intricate cuts, shuffles, and turns necessary to follow the puck. Playing with Goal Skates eliminates the rocking motion a young goaltender will have if he/she is using Player Skates due its curved blade.

CHEST/SHOULDER PADS. The designs of CHEST/SHOULDER PADS have been enhanced remarkably over the years. In order to meet all the important protection and mobility needs of the modern day goaltender, this piece of equipment includes a lot of overlapping protection and extremely lightweight materials. The new designs have assisted in preventing injuries to the arms, abdomen, ribs, and chest areas.

There is a critical element that *must be addressed* when dealing with a CHEST/SHOULER PAD. Often, it is *adjusted incorrectly*. This piece of equipment cannot be purchased haphazardly off the shelf and be expected to fit properly.

Tip #1 - It must be adjusted so that it *sits firmly against the chest;* adjust the waist strap to meet this need.

Tip #2 - It must be adjusted so that it *sits UP high enough* to reach the lower part of the neck; adjust the length of the back strap to meet this need.

The **CHEST/SHOULDER PAD** should wrap around the goaltender's waist; it should protect the sides and rib areas when it is adjusted properly (See Tips #1, 2). It MUST be *worn inside* the goaltender's pants in order to accomplish these two important adjustments!

SPECIAL NOTE: The largest mistake that is made when purchasing goaltender equipment is that most *buyers* choose hockey pants (or goaltending pants) that are far too small! Goaltender pants need to be large enough to permit the CHEST/SHOULDER PAD to be worn *inside*!

ARM/SHOULDER PADS (alternate option): It is imperative for goaltenders to cut and sew extra padding into existing ARM/SHOULDER PADS to gain a sufficient amount of protection. Even today's most modern and protective units on the market may require customization.

Tip #3 - Obtaining used hockey pants that can be cut apart and sewn into valuable *add-ons* may be the difference in being a timid, hesitant goaltender as compared to a very confident and aggressive puck stopper!

Goaltenders have to do whatever it takes to protect every part of the body with custom made pieces if their existing equipment is not protecting them effectively!

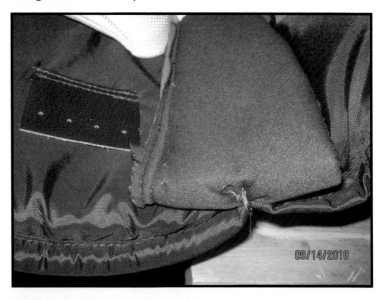

BREAKING IN GOALTENDER EQUIPMENT

The days of soaking the goaltender equipment in various leather conditioning products to preserve and to soften the leather for easier break-in purposes have *come and gone,* thankfully. The quality and design of goaltender equipment has come a long way since the days we experienced when, at the end of game, one *brown* goal pad would be heavier and shaped differently than the other!

In fact, it was simple to discover a goaltender's style by observing the amount of water that was drenched inside the goal pads. Today, lightweight modern materials require less and less pre-use attention.

TRAPPER. The TRAPPER remains the chief product that requires plenty of attention during the hockey season. It needs to be *broken-in* on several levels before it can be considered ready for important use.

Tip #1 - The pocket of the TRAPPER must be broken in sufficiently. A goaltender must be capable of closing it completely and easily without any restrictions or stiffness. The leather portion of the TRAPPER's pocket must receive special attention right from its first use.

SPECIAL NOTE: To assist in the quick and correct method of softening and breaking in the pocket area, it helps to use a special *hammer* called a *Ball Peen Hammer*!

What Is A Ball Peen Hammer? One end of the hammer is *rounded off*! Use the rounded end of the hammer to hit the entire pocket area of the TRAPPER aggressively and repeatedly while it is being worn properly. Spend one evening hitting the TRAPPER's pocket simulating many, many pucks being caught, while watching your favorite hockey team on the television. Using a ball peen hammer method while practicing opening and closing the TRAPPER quickly produces one that is broken in properly.

CAUTION: DO NOT overdo the strength of each hit; regulate the impact the hand will receive.

Tip #2 - The next most important aspect of taking great care of the TRAPPER can be summed up by responding correctly to the question, *How should the TRAPPER be stored when it is not in use?* The TRAPPER's pocket MUST remain *fully open*; it should never appear to close FLAT like a pancake.

It is important to ALWAYS keep a softball strapped inside the TRAPPER's pocket in order to guarantee a perfectly wide open TRAPPER!

This can be done easily by using:

- an adjustable belt
- a length of rope
- a long velcro strap (which we believe is the *most effective* method)

A little help from My Friends!

REMEMBER: THE TRAPPER SHOULD NEVER BE THROWN INTO THE EQUIPMENT BAG INSENSITIVELY!

Tip #3 - Developing the TRAPPER into a perfect extension of a goaltender's hand is extremely important! In addition to catching, trapping, and covering pucks, it plays an essential role in puck-handling, passing, and shooting! Puck-handling is a skill that every goaltender MUST add to their personal *goaltender system*. Being able to grasp the lower portion of the goal stick firmly with the TRAPPER will greatly assist in a hard, accurate pass and shot (see Chapter 10).

The part of the TRAPPER that is most important when a goaltender shoots the puck is the *TIP OF THE WEB*. If the *TIP* area remains hard and very firm, the goaltender will have a difficult time grabbing onto the goal stick. Using a *ball peen hammer* will be most effective in softening this area too.

A dilemma can be created by softening the *TIP* area too severely. As well, the TRAPPER needs to have a large, strong web area so that it will not break down when pucks from blistering slap shots are caught! It is important for a goaltender to be attentive to this point when he/she works on the **TIP OF THE WEB.**

A goaltender MUST be able to catch every puck that comes near the TRAPPER! It is important for a goaltender to adjust all the finger straps so it becomes tight around the hand. Each shot that a goaltender catches prevents a rebound; catching the puck gives teammates confidence in a goaltender's puck stopping abilities.

Catching pucks also provides teammates with more strategic options (e.g., the goaltender is in full control of the play when the puck is inside the TRAPPER); if the puck just hits the TRAPPER and falls to the ice, rebounds and puck possession can be offered carelessly to opposing players! When the TRAPPER is treated properly, it will return the favor exponentially to the goaltender. A properly treated TRAPPER will assist in several **OUTSTANDING SAVES,** not to mention the rich amount of quality passes to teammates and zone-clearing shots that will occur!

GOAL PADS (LEG PADS). The most expensive investment goaltenders require is what protects their legs - GOAL PADS. They come in many different styles and colors.

Proper fitting GOAL PADS will help goaltenders be more successful in and around the crease area. Goaltenders MUST be able to:

- skate forwards, backwards, and sideways
- go down onto their knees and get back onto their feet quickly
- drop to one knee while leaving the other off the ice

None of these skills can be done effectively with GOAL PADS that are either too small or too big.

STYLES: There are three basic styles of GOAL PADS:

1. Butterfly Style: This style is designed for goaltenders that want the Flat-Look-Face of the GOAL PAD to be along the ice in order to maximize coverage along the bottom of the ice. Butterfly Style GOAL PADS can be identified by the support provided to the inner leg channel.

2. Stand-Up Style: This style is designed for goaltenders that prefer a more traditional technique by taking away more of the upper net.

3. Hybrid Style: This style is designed for goaltenders that prefer more of a mixture between stand-up style and butterfly style.

Sizing Standards: It is important to note that GOAL PADS must now conform to NHL and International Ice Hockey sizing standards. They must not exceed the width of 11 inches. They have to protect goaltenders, but they cannot have additional advantages. They now come with a *plus one, two, etc. thigh rise*. GOAL PADS with a *plus one, two, etc. thigh rise* provide goaltenders with a superior butterfly (e.g., closing holes).

Customization: GOAL PADS can be customized by almost any manufacturer. Having Custom-Spec GOAL PADS over Stock GOAL PADS allows goaltenders to have the options to suit and fit a specific style in net. Once fitted properly with GOAL PADS, the goaltenders' knees should lay behind the middle knee roll. The Top of the GOAL PAD should be *no higher* than two-thirds of the way up the thigh of the leg.

Where They Are Made: GOAL PADS that are made in Canada are generally the Pro-Series, Professional level pads. The Pro-Series are the best quality GOAL PADS on the market. The Pro-Series GOAL PADS offer the best performance on the ice. Most manufacturers use the best quality materials for constructing Pro-Series GOAL PADS because they are used by goaltenders that play high levels of hockey and/or use them almost every day. A goaltender that plays high levels of hockey or wants the Professional look and feel should purchase a set of Pro-Series GOAL PADS.

IMPORTANT NOTE: There are many manufacturers that have decided to go overseas to produce GOAL PADS. This is more cost efficient for both manufacturers and the consumers. This allows for a growing child or a goaltender that just plays once in a while to have a great set of GOAL PADS that can still be cost effective. The materials used are of less quality than the Pro-Series. However, they still offer the performance of new style GOAL PADS.

DIFFERENT STYLES - A DEEPER LOOK: Many GOAL PAD manufacturers develop different styles. One style is built much *stiffer* than others which allows for a *stronger pad*. This style allows goaltenders to execute a pure Butterfly Style. This style moves more easily and rotates on the goaltenders' legs as if they were not attached.

Manufacturers now include more break points on GOAL PADS; this allows the GOAL PADS to conform more to the goaltenders' bodies. GOAL PADS that have break points provide goaltenders with more flexibility in the pad. This style that has break points is classified as a Hybrid Style. The break points can really help goaltenders with their movements on the ice. A set of GOAL PADS with break points allows goaltenders to have a softer feel around their legs.

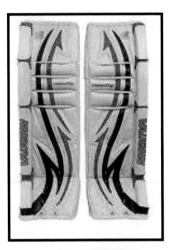

An Important Point from Coach Brent Bradford and Coach Vic LeMire:

Properly fitting Goal Pads allow for smooth, explosive movements in and around the crease area!

Leg Channels: There are different types of Leg Channels.

1. Closed Leg Channel: A *closed leg channel* (e.g., one that is closer to the goaltender's leg) allows for more control with the body. Many goaltenders prefer this style because it allows for better movement in net while still remaining close to their legs.

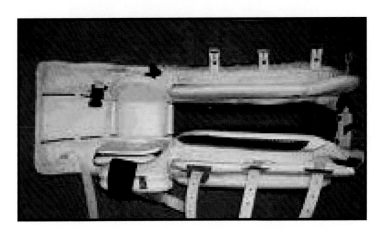

2. Open Leg Channel: An *open leg channel* allows goaltenders to have a loose feel around their bodies, thus making skating drills in the crease feel like nothing is attached to their legs.

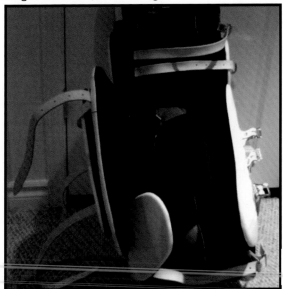

An *open leg channel* greatly assists with the butterfly. It allows goaltenders to have flat and closed face GOAL PADS along the ice.

Boot Channels: There are different types of Boot/Skate Channels.

1. Flat Boot Channel: A Flat Boot Channel allows goaltenders to have great rotation. The GOAL PADS sit up higher on the leg.

2. Curved Boot Channel: A *Curved Boot Channel* allows goaltenders to have a close and snug feel to their skates.

A *Pre-curved Boot Channel* provides goaltenders with the steady feel when they are exploding into the butterfly position (e.g., cutting deeper into the ice with skates becomes much easier).

Knee Cradles: There are different types of Knee Cradles.

1. Closed Knee Cradle: A *Closed Knee Cradle* provides goaltenders with a *lock-in-feel*. This allows goaltenders to sit closer to the ice while still having the protection of the *stackers*. Having a *Closed Knee Cradle* also allows goaltenders to have their GOAL PADS stay on their knees while they move.

2. Open Knee Cradle: An *Open Knee Cradle* provides goaltenders with free space around their knees. This is very beneficial when goaltenders are moving in the crease.

When goaltenders are in the butterfly position, the *Open Knee Cradle* allows them to have a *closed* and *flat-to-the-ice butterfly*.

Front-Face-Looks: There are different types of Front-Face-Looks.

1. Front Roles: An older, but still very popular look is one with Front Roles. GOAL PADS with Front Roles provide goaltenders with great rebound control. Once the puck hits the GOAL PADS, it slows down providing goaltenders with opportunities to cover it up or clear it away. Mastering rebound control with this type is extremely advantageous.

2. Flat-Face: GOAL PADS with a Flat-Face allow goaltenders to have quick rebound control. Manufacturers are now using high-density foam in GOAL PADS; this provides goaltenders with a superb way of controlling rebounds. When goaltenders master a Flat-Faced set of GOAL PADS, they will have quick and superb rebound control. Pucks will go where they should (away from potential shooters) when rebound control is mastered by goaltenders!

When Purchasing GOAL PADS: It is important to determine what style of GOAL PADS will best suit the goaltender (customized options are important to pay attention to, e.g., Knee Cradle, Boot Channel, etc.). Figuring out what level the goaltender will play is a key factor in determining the quality of the GOAL PADS that will be required.

CHAPTER 3 - MENTAL PREPARATION

Goaltending is a **Thinking Man's Game**! The following goaltending situations are ALL masterful examples of well-trained goaltenders demonstrating the physical aspects of their games.

- Making that great glove save!
- Providing intelligent puck-handling on a moment's notice!
- EXPLODING out rapidly to challenge a shot!
- Controlling a rebound perfectly!
- Sliding across the crease to make that mind-blowing blocker save!

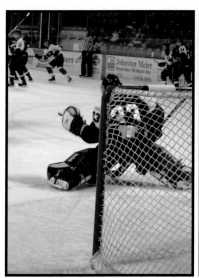 

There is a part of a goaltender's performance that cannot be observed by the naked eye during each and every game. What we are describing here is the *other* extremely critical part of being a great goaltender; it is the exceedingly valuable *mental preparation program* that must be developed.

There are many mental aspects to the game that every serious goaltender must discover. Each mental aspect will be *custom-made* on a personal level. They are created and strengthened over many hockey seasons as goaltenders strive to successfully implement them into their personal *goaltending system*.

The mental aspects are as follows:

1. Mental Imagery Databases

Goaltenders have unknowingly begun to develop their own *Mental Imagery Database* from the time they stopped their very first puck. However, today's best goaltenders in the game of hockey learn very quickly how to *file* each particular save into his/her own *Mental Imagery Database* for future recovery.

Various *Mental Imagery Database* titles may include:

a) **Breakaways**
  - How I used a Poke Check
  - Setting up Left- or Right-handed shooters
  - Forcing the shooter to shoot 5-hole

b) **Great Glove Saves**
  - *Stealing* a sure goal away
  - Picking off a screened shot
  - Grabbing a one-time shot

c) **Playing 2 on 1's**
  - Taking the shooter
  - Forcing the shooter to *bite*, setting him up
  - Making that great save on a pass across

     . . . as well as many other special game situations.

Note To Goaltenders: *All of these game situations will be discussed in detail throughout the later chapters!*

Goaltender's Personal "Great Save" Video/DVD: When goaltenders prepare to play a game, they work very hard on their physical skills in practice. There is no short cut to success as skills such as mobility, skating, rebound control, and more are truly important game preparation strategies. Equally important are the mental preparation skills that every goaltender must learn to include during their game preparations.

Developing a positive attitude throughout all your game day activities is the key to *SHOWING UP to play*! **Coach Brent Bradford and Coach Vic LeMire** strongly recommend the daily use of a personal edited video tape to show a series of a goaltender's GREAT SAVES!

All season long, goaltenders should strive to collect edited versions of their best performances saved to a Video Tape/DVD that can be accessible for personal use. They should replay all the jaw-dropping saves as often as they like ultimately knowing that they will be etched in their memory bank for retrieval on a moment's notice.

The added value of a properly edited Great Save Video Tape/DVD is the making of several copies for distribution to those many Colleges and Universities that strive to recruit a special goaltender on scholarship! The NCAA and Canadian University varsity hockey coaches gladly accept short, edited versions of game performances, but they simply do not have the valuable time to watch whole games. Goaltenders must select specific skills that show great save successes including Breakaways, Mobility Saves, Proper Positioning, and Great Glove Saves to name a few! *May ALL your saves be GREAT ones!*

2. Game Preparation

Athletes from every sport indicate how important the special *game day routines* are to them! Repeating specific tasks brings the mind to a *familiar successful space*.

a) Game Day - Morning

NOTE TO GOALTENDERS: It is important to begin the *GAME DAY* by replaying the *Mental Imagery Databases* in your mind. It is as simple as closing your eyes and re-living any of your past outstanding saves in each category. Re-live the play from the start to its amazingly successful conclusion.

b) Game Day - At The Hockey Arena

Goaltenders must make the *Mental Imagery Databases* part of their everyday pre-game preparation. Find those quiet moments to reflect on . . . *just how great of a goaltender you truly are!*

GOALTENDERS: Find a quiet section of the arena (e.g., up in the seats, down the hallway, or in an additional empty locker room). Remember those Great Saves! Open your eyes with a newly found positive attitude and **keep your mind focused** on all those outstanding saves you have recently made. **Get your game face on!** NOW, you have become an *Educated, Game-Prepared Goaltender*!

c) Game Day - Getting In The Zone!

TIME FOR SOME *HIGH LEVEL* THINKING: The term **autotelic** is used to describe people who are internally driven. People who have **autotelic** personalities exhibit a sense of purpose and curiosity; they demonstrate strong skills surrounding *leadership* and *motivation*.

People who have **autotelic** personalities are highly self-directed and independent; they are not easily manipulated by external threats or rewards. At the same time, they are exceedingly involved with everything around them; they are fully occupied with the task at hand.

People with **autotelic** personalities encourage growth. They have greater preferences for **"high-action opportunities and high-skills situations that stimulate them"** (e.g., important playoff hockey games) than those without **autotelic** personalities. It is during such high-challenge and high-skills situations that people with **autotelic** personalities are most likely to **get in the zone** and enter the **flow state**.

IMPORTANT QUESTION: Do you think a hockey coach would rather have a goaltender **with** or **without** an **autotelic personality**? Why?

The ZONE: There is a special mental **"ZONE"** that a goaltender must learn to enter in order for his/her performances to progress to the highest levels of hockey! It is a magical and special place when performance is exceptional and consistent, automatic and flowing. An elite athlete is able to ignore all the pressures and let his/her body deliver the performance that has been learned so well. The *zone*, which refers to an athlete's highest peak of achievement, characterizes a state in which an athlete performs to the best of his/her ability.

In every advanced level of sport, the most successful athletes bring their own *"zone preparations"* (e.g., *wired in*, *in the groove*, or *keeping your head in the game*.)

TYING IT TOGETHER: The feeling of being *in the zone* is identical to the idea of *flow*. The *flow state* is an optimal state of *intrinsic motivation* (i.e., being fully occupied with the task at hand); an individual is completely involved in an activity for its own sake. Every single action, movement, and thought follows inevitably from the previous one (i.e., all actions flow from one to the next). The individual's whole being is involved, and he/she employs his/her skills to the utmost potential.

ATTENTION GOALTENDERS: When one is in the *flow state*, he/she is completely immersed in a feeling of energized focus on the **one task at hand** and, without making the conscious decision to do so, loses awareness of all other things (e.g., time, people, and other external distractions). This occurs because all of the individual's attention in the *flow state* is on the task at hand; there is no more attention to be shared with other thoughts (e.g., what am I going to do after the hockey game?)

Goaltenders, how would you answer the following questions? During your hockey games …

1. … do you have a sense of personal *control* over the hockey game?
2. … is the hockey game *intrinsically* rewarding?
3. … are you fully absorbed into the hockey game and able to narrow the focus of awareness down to the hockey game itself, (i.e., *the emergence of action awareness*)?
4. … are you *concentrating* on the most important items (do you have a high degree of concentration on a limited field of attention, i.e., *stopping pucks*)?

**An Important Message from
Coach Brent Bradford and Coach Vic LeMire:**

You must find a way to always get "in the zone" and enter the "flow state" during your hockey games if you truly want to reach the highest levels of hockey!

NOW, GET YOUR GAME FACE ON!

CHAPTER 4 - HEAD SHOTS

Goaltenders are bound to receive plenty of head shots throughout their hockey careers. The only time goaltenders' helmets or masks should be hit by a puck is during competitive game action. Head shots should not occur during team practices and/or game warm-ups from inside the blue line (shots from outside the blue line can be taken as **high** and **hard** as a teammate chooses). Realistically, there will be times during team practices and/or game warm-ups when a puck is accidentally shot **high** and **hard** toward a goaltender's head.

THE *HEAD SHOT* RULE: A teammate gets *one chance* to shoot the puck accidentally **high** and **hard** toward a goaltender's head during a practice or a game warm-up from inside the blue line. If this rule is not followed by the goaltenders' teammates and coaches, goaltenders need to take *action*.

TIME FOR ACTION - *TAKE ONE!* When head shots that are taken by the goaltenders' teammates become problematic and a consistent occurrence, it should be dealt with immediately. Goaltenders MUST first express their concerns regarding head shots to the Coaching Staff. A quality Coaching Staff will address this issue in a meaningful and effective manner.

TIME FOR ACTION - *TAKE TWO!* If however, the Coaching Staff does not consider consistent head shots during a practice and/or a game warm-up to pose a problem (e.g., possible year-ending injury), then goaltenders have two traditional options to choose from:

1. **Step Out** - Goaltenders can simply choose to step out of the net when a specific teammate that consistently chooses to shoot **high** and **hard** from inside the blue line is skating down the ice during a drill. This will provide that teammate with an open net to shoot at. He/she will soon find out it is not that beneficial to have to always shoot at an open net (e.g., shooting accuracy will not improve).

2. **Return The Favour** - Goaltenders can simply return the favour of getting hit in the head with a shot by (1) returning the puck **high** and **hard** back to the teammate that displays such little respect during practices and/or game warm-ups, and/or (2) key in on that teammate during game-like drills and let him/her know what the Goal Stick feels like on the ankles!

Often times, goaltenders need to look after themselves. During practices and/or game warm-ups, it is imperative for goaltenders to address the issue of head shots for their own safety and for the needs of the team (e.g., a team with a goaltender on the injured-reserve list poses a negative situation to the Coaching Staff).

CHAPTER 5 - SLUMPS AND WINNING STREAKS

All Goaltenders Will Experience Them! Throughout any given hockey season, goaltenders at all levels will inevitably go through (1) **SLUMPS** and (2) **WINNING STREAKS** (i.e., (1) a span of games when more goals are scored against than usual on a goaltender leading to potential losses and (2) a span of games when everything seems to be going right and a team wins).

1 - WHY DO SLUMPS EXIST? Slumps exist when goaltenders lose confidence and/or when they stray from their necessary off-ice mental and physical preparations. They lose the special attention to the finer details which are required in maintaining the *elite* levels of successful goaltending. This loss of preparation and details always leads to pucks finding their way into goal nets on more than the average occasion.

During these times, goaltenders let goals in that do not seem to be the type of goals that usually enter the nets behind them (e.g., goals from behind the goal line, bouncing pucks from long distances, and simple shots from the point). All it takes to fuel a slump is a goaltender that has decided to overlook the finer details of goaltending while allowing a weak goal to enter the net (e.g., not placing his/her stick blade firmly on the ice between the legs when making a butterfly save).

HOW TO HANDLE A SLUMP IN A POSITIVE MANNER! What separates *elite* goaltenders from others is how *elite* goaltenders, that are extremely educated in the Game of Hockey, are capable of accepting a slump as part of the game while not at all being satisfied with its existence. *Elite* goaltenders are able to deal with a slump in a positive manner and take action to overcome it.

In order to become an *elite* goaltender, one must search for effective strategies to implement when he/she is beginning to observe the signs of a slump. Refocusing on the most specific goaltender skills (e.g., hugging the post properly) will help enable the goaltender to mentally prepare him/herself to end the slump and to begin the process of winning games once again. Goaltenders that are experiencing a slump MUST get back to the *basics of goaltending* quickly in order to put the slump to rest. Most importantly, *elite* goaltenders must produce a very strong work ethic amongst his/her teammates and demonstrate that they are willing to work extremely hard and to become determined to change things around! They must show that they are not willing to accept a slump lightly and they are leaders steering their respective teams into a positive direction!

2 - WHY DO WINNING STREAKS EXIST? There are times during a hockey season when a goaltender's team finds ways to win hockey games (with the help of the goaltenders of course!). During the course of a winning streak, goaltenders make terrific mind-blowing saves while the forwards and defensemen score highlight-reel goals. This leads to a strong attitude of quiet invincibility or at least constructive confidence amongst the whole team!

During these times, goaltenders usually save shots at a higher than average rate and their individual statistics rise dramatically (e.g., GAA, Saves %). All it takes to fuel a winning streak is a strong game by a team, including the goaltender, and a total team effort toward playing the team's system while getting a few breaks from the Hockey Gods along the way!

HOW TO HANDLE A WINNING STREAK IN A POSITIVE MANNER! What separates *elite* goaltenders from others is how *elite* goaltenders, that are extremely educated in the Game of Hockey, are capable of accepting a winning streak as part of the game while not getting too high on him/herself and becoming overconfident with its existence. *Elite* goaltenders are able to deal with a winning streak in a positive yet humble manner.

A team's winning streak is the perfect opportunity for educated goaltenders to set higher performance goals with all their off-ice physical and mental training programs. Extra work on shooting the puck in practice or staying on the ice after practice to put in some extra work in order to increase strength and endurance are just a couple examples of how goaltenders can reach higher levels of performance!

In order to become an *elite* goaltender, one must search for effective strategies to implement when he/she is beginning to observe the signs of a winning streak. Extra hard work and remaining focused on the most specific goaltender skills (e.g., making smart passes) will help enable the goaltender to remain mentally prepared to continue the winning streak while striving to keep potential slumps from occurring.

**An Important Consideration from
Coach Brent Bradford and Coach Vic LeMire:**

*Goaltenders MUST understand that SLUMPS and WINNING STREAKS
can be cyclical throughout the duration of a hockey season ... in order
to reach elite status; goaltenders MUST strive to increase the frequency
of WINNING STREAKS and decrease the frequency of SLUMPS!
Goaltenders MUST remain focused on the most specific goaltending
skills at all times during the hockey season!*
*DO NOT GET
TOO HIGH DURING WINNING STREAKS
OR
TOO LOW DURING SLUMPS!*

A Bradford/LeMire Homework Assignment

*After each one of your hockey games, write
down three key saves you made. Include a
descriptive overview of what was happening a
few seconds prior to making the save and
make note of what save selection you chose;
explain why. Also, write down how your
teammates and the opposing players reacted
to each save. By doing this for the entire
season, you will develop a heightened
awareness of how GREAT SAVES can affect a
game's outcome and how they can influence
the players around you (i.e., positively and
negatively).*

CHAPTER 6 - HOCKEY PARENTS/GUARDIANS

The most important part of every goaltender's life will always be his or her "Parents/Guardians!" Most goaltenders are truly blessed as they have extremely forgiving, encouraging, dedicated, and loving parents.

PARENTITIS: There is a large segment of hockey parents/guardians who have unfortunately contracted a dangerous and damaging *syndrome* called **PARENTITIS**!

One of our very dear friends, Mr. Roy Henderson of Global Sports, formerly an NHL scout with the Philadelphia Flyers, created the incredibly descriptive term called PARENTITIS. He applied this term correctly to some very identifiable hockey parents who have contracted this *syndrome*.

Characteristics of PARENTITIS are:

✓ Parents/Guardians who hold extremely unrealistic dreams of grandeur for their young hockey players

✓ Parents/Guardians who show despicable displays of pressure and embarrassment to themselves and to their young hockey players

They are easy to identify in and around the hockey arena by the screams, the curses, the loud and outrageous comments, and the intimidating conduct they bring to every game.

The children of these imposing parents are unfortunately headed for heartbreak and disappointment; every coach and scout will hear of these **trouble parents/guardians** through the **hockey grapevine**! Every hockey team will begin to recognize the parents/guardians with PARENTITIS and will avoid the pending confrontations that are sure to develop by deciding to never allow PARENTITIS into their organization.

Parents/Guardians MUST learn to become **silent partners** in their young goaltenders' careers! They need to become a "FAN". They must support and encourage their children from a distance. Goaltenders must become extroverted, independent individuals who, with guidance from background parental support, shall face each and every challenge on their own.

TIPS FOR GOALTENDERS (only):

✓ Speak with the coach and have regular meetings with him/her.
✓ Search out the various scouts attending your games and introduce yourself with a strong, firm, and confident handshake.

As a successful goaltender, it is important to quickly become a strong, responsible individual and to demonstrate to everyone in the hockey business that **YOU** are in charge of your hockey career and life.

The DREADED RIDE HOME! With a combined 60-plus years of experiences of coaching, mentoring, and guiding hockey players, we have developed a very unique and valuable perspective of the special love and care that brings out the *best* in a goaltender! Unfortunately, during that same time span, we have also witnessed some of the most dreadful and unbearable parenting practices imaginable brought onto hard working goaltenders.

WHICH ARE YOU? There are added pressures brought into a Hockey Parent/Child relationship. The pressures being described are NOT part of a family's everyday growth pattern. *Would you know what these pressures are?*

We hope to raise awareness and to create solutions for many parents/guardians who make terrible mistakes that cause psychological damage to young children. To be very truthful and blunt, some parents/guardians *take all the FUN out of playing hockey* for their children!

First, we give you the "location" ... a PRISON ... a place with locks and a strait jacket (i.e., seatbelt) to ensure containment, virtually no method of escape. Yes, it is the "Family Car!" Young hockey players obtain their first taste of the *terror* usually on the way to their hockey game or practice in the *Family Car*. These players are exposed to many forceful commands and unreasonable demands right out of their own driveway before they have even stepped onto the ice!

Comments like:

✓ "You better not be late on the ice for practice!" says one father … (This occurs even though the father arrived home late to pick his/her young hockey player up!)
✓ "Remember, I am paying all this money for you to play hockey … so I better see you work extra hard out there!"
✓ "You make sure that you do what I tell you in this game. Never mind what the coach says!"

These are just a few of the *regular* commands that are forced into the minds and hearts of young hockey players. There are many more verbally a*busive*, one-way conversations that take place in this situation. Parents/Guardians have, what amounts to, a truly CAPTIVE AUDIENCE in the *Family Car*. Unfortunately, there are some parents/guardians who seem to take complete advantage of this situation!

Now The Game Is Over! Coming to the game after a hard day at work or at home, some parents/guardians release their frustrations with yelling and screaming in the stands. This is PARENTITIS. It is these same adults that cannot wait to get their young hockey players into their cars to ***GRILL them all over again***! (*Hockey sounds so FUN to this point - doesn't it?*)

- ✓ "Why is that other kid playing on YOUR line? He is terrible!"
- ✓ "You came off the ice after only 30 seconds ... why don't you stay out there longer?
- ✓ "That coach of yours just really does not know how to coach properly!
- ✓ "Why did you freeze the puck up, play it next time, do not listen to what your coach said!"

Tips For Parents/Guardians: You are rightly justified to try to help your goaltender develop the hockey skills necessary to compete successfully at high levels. You are also expected and qualified to keep the learning atmosphere completely **healthy** and **enjoyable**. It is *so* much simpler to teach someone with *honey* than with *vinegar*. It is true; each child requires feedback and support (both educational and emotional...not to mention financial support is needed at all times!).

The **EDUCATIONAL** feedback of playing hockey is most often best left to hockey coaches. It is quite proper and beneficial for coaches and parents/guardians to meet several times per season to discuss exactly what the projected teaching plan will be for a young hockey player.

- ✓ Make this a "Joint" effort!
- ✓ Develop a **PERSONAL TEACHING PROGRAM** designed by you and your coaches whereby you both agree to monitor, encourage, and reward each and every accomplishment that your young goaltender successfully completes.

✓ Have various attainable *goals* set ahead of time with realistic chances of success.
✓ Do not expect to see your child become the fastest skater after only a few practices!

Set up *performance goals* for each practice that will enhance a goaltender's skills by using *BABY STEPS*! This will produce such delight of accomplishment to the goaltender that he/she just cannot wait to get out onto the ice again for the next practice. Honestly … this method WORKS for all hockey players from *Little Squirts* to *NHL Professionals*.

Now that you are in the car with your young goaltender, it is most important to speak heavily of all his/her great improvements he/she recently accomplished! If necessary, WAIT until several hours have passed to bring up ANY problems or ideas about something that he/she should strive to improve on or to correct!

YES … areas of concern must be addressed! However, *timing* and *tactical presentation* can make all the difference in the world as to how your child receives your important information!

TECHNOLOGY TOOLS: In the EDUCATIONAL aspect of your goaltender's development, many of you have discovered the GREAT advent of the *video camera* as a teaching tool! It is an *awesome tool!* When it is used correctly, it has the capability to promote and to encourage your goaltender. Every family should develop a **"GREAT SAVE" DVD** and have many copies available for distribution to hockey coaches and scouts (e.g., Junior/College/University).

A **DVD** of the *GREATEST SAVES* is the perfect medium for a goaltender to analyze before every game.

Note To The Goaltender:

➢ Know that you are GREAT!
➢ Prepare for each game properly!
➢ Learn to enjoy the positive background support of your *Game Educated Parents/Guardians*!

A video camera is extremely effective when it is used as a teaching aid … but **BEWARE** … it also offers its own lethal problems when it is used in an inappropriate manner! If a parent/guardian is sitting a goaltender down to point out **MISTAKES** being made all the time, he/she is, in fact, emphasizing these mistakes over and over again! Are you able to understand how quickly your goaltender will decide to make every excuse in the world up in order to avoid watching his/her hockey game videos?

AN IMPORTANT POINT TO CONSIDER: Have you ever noticed how *EXCITED* a goaltender becomes when he/she observes a freeze frame snap-shot of him/herself *in game action*? It is never threatening ... only breathtaking to see the gracefulness and special effort that is frozen in time ... *NO MISTAKES HERE* ... only great efforts and super memories!

A *VIDEO TAPE/DVD* can illustrate a plethora of mistakes on almost every shift during a game - *if that is what you want to point out, it can easily be done*. Using the rewind button with slow motion just adds to the degradation of the moment! The proper way to *TEACH* at home using video tapes of a goaltender's performance is to **select at least four segments of GREAT PERFORMANCES** to discuss before even trying to examine one segment of mistakes!

Using the **Bradford's Goal Academy 4:1 Feedback Ratio** (i.e., four positive comments to every negative comment) will enable goaltenders to remain positive in the most conducive learning environments!

REMEMBER: *Honey ATTRACTS MORE THAN Vinegar*!

EMOTIONAL feedback is either (1) the *glue* that produces a lifetime of great memories and incredible FUN for your goaltender's life **OR** (2) the *pain* that causes them to RUN AWAY from the great sport of hockey which could potentially turn them toward making negative choices (e.g., immoral acts, drug use, etc.).

Do you realize that it is impossible for someone to break into a neighbour's home or to do drugs with a neighbour's family member if he/she is *ON THE ICE* having *FUN* playing hockey?

Note To Parents/Guardians: The following is a taste of reality that we hope each hockey family seriously considers throughout the years!

- ✓ How important is hockey in your family's life - Really?
- ✓ Was it necessary to swear at your goaltender because you were angry that a goal went in (even when you strive to teach him/her not to swear ... what message do you think you are sending)?
- ✓ Why throw a hockey stick outside into a field after a game your child just played because he/she made a mistake on the ice?
- ✓ Is your goaltender's respect toward you important to you at all?

REMEMBER: Make sure your young hockey player knows how pleased you are with his/her effort. Explain to him/her that all the hard work he/she is doing will result in positive outcomes. Tell him/her about all the GREAT efforts he/she displayed; he/she will become so hungry for more compliments and will enjoy the positive conversation.

What a teachable moment you have the ability to create! You can reveal to your child the true reason for playing hockey! Parents, if you cannot provide a calm and positive atmosphere for your child when traveling to and/or from the hockey arena, ***GET someone else to drive him/her*** to games and practices! Hockey players should be so happy to jump into a car and explain to you how much FUN the game was ... and to THANK YOU for driving them to the game!

Questions To Ponder:

✓ When was the last time your child thanked you for helping him/her play hockey?

✓ Has your child ever asked you not to attend any more games due to your embarrassing profanity in a sports environment surrounded by children?

✓ When was the last time you went outside and practiced alongside your child and gave him/her a high-five?

We pray this chapter hits home with those who really need to hear it! Have FUN and truly enjoy each other through the wonderful hockey years! They will go by fast ... and you will WISH them back!

That is a ...
Coach Brent Bradford and Coach Vic LeMire Guarantee!

A Bradford/LeMire Homework Assignment

When you watch and study NHL goaltenders during game action, try to key in on all the shots that miss the net when the shooter is coming down on an angle. Examine where the goaltender is standing while in the Ready (SET) Position. Make notes of what you observe. Why do you think the puck missed the net? What can you learn from watching these types of NHL game situations? How do NHL goaltenders play angle shots most effectively?

PART TWO

PREPARING TO BECOME A GOALTENDER

CHAPTER 7 - PRE-GAME WARM-UP - *Are You Ready?*

ATTENTION GOALTENDERS: Prior to your pre-game warm-up, you MUST take your equipment into the dressing room and set it up neatly in your designated stall. By setting up your equipment in the stall tidily as opposed to throwing it around haphazardly (which can often be found in dressing rooms), you are demonstrating a great deal of pride in your equipment and you are sending a non-verbal message to your coaches and teammates that you are focused in on the game; *IT SHOWS YOU TRULY CARE ABOUT YOUR TEAM AND YOUR ENVIRONMENT!*

AFTER THE EQUIPMENT IS SET UP NEATLY IN THE STALL. Warming up prior to a game takes a lot of preparation. A goaltender MUST begin his/her warm-up well before he/she steps onto the ice. A proper warm-up for a goaltender consists of a variety of components, including; *elevating the heart rate and increasing blood flow to the muscles, stretching, performing hand-eye coordination exercises*, and *feeling the puck*. We will now go into specific details surrounding these four major elements that MUST become part of a goaltender's pre-game warm-up.

1. Elevating The Heart Rate And Increasing Blood Flow To The Muscles. A very common pre-game warm-up strategy that occurs off the ice is progressing from a light jog into more vigorous running-type exercises near the dressing room or in the stands. Goaltenders need to elevate their heart rates and increase the blood flow to their muscles so that they are fully prepared to exercise at a high level and to be able to stretch their bodies effectively and efficiently. *IT IS EXTREMELY IMPORTANT TO EMPLOY PROGRESSIVE EXERCISES DURING THIS PART OF THE PRE-GAME WARM-UP IN ORDER TO PREVENT UNWANTED INJURIES.*

2. Stretching. Following a few minutes of elevating the heart rate (e.g., jogging, running, etc.), goaltenders MUST engage in a stretching routine that will allow the major muscles to perform under the most demanding game situations that will occur usually in an hour or so. This segment of the pre-game warm-up MUST include stretching all the major muscle groups entirely.

3. Performing Hand-Eye Coordination Exercises. After the goaltenders have elevated their heart rate and stretched out their major muscle groups, they can now begin to concentrate on their specific task-at-hand; engaging in hand-eye coordination exercises that simulate stopping a puck. We highly recommend that goaltenders engage in the Racquetball Drill during this segment of the pre-game warm-up (see Chapter 8). By employing this drill, goaltenders will start to think about their job of stopping pucks and will begin to concentrate on the finer details of hand-eye coordination.

4. Feeling The Puck. Once the goaltender steps onto the ice for the next segment of the pre-game warm-up, he/she must be ready to step into the net to stop pucks after a few minutes of stretching out and performing some goaltender-specific skating drills to get comfortable with all his/her equipment on.

Goaltenders MUST face shots during pre-game warm-up that allow them to feel the puck and to become comfortable in and around the crease area. They should have opportunities to stop long shots, pass-outs, pucks traveling around the back boards, etc.

Once the goaltender completes this portion of the pre-game warm-up, he/she should be ready to be the difference-maker in the game; he/she MUST be fully prepared to stop every puck during the game with precision and grace!

ATTENTION GOALTENDERS: In order to be fully prepared to compete during a game at your highest potential, you MUST be warmed up entirely. We suggest that you take some time to create your pre-game warm-up which should include the ideas and strategies noted above. DO NOT let your team down just because you never took the time prior to the game to become fully warmed up … and DO NOT set yourself up for an injury due to an ineffective pre-game warm-up!

Did You Know …

The first goaltender to wear a face mask regularly in the NHL was Montreal's Jacques Plante. After a shot broke his nose in 1959, he decided to wear one. He paved the way for all goaltenders; now every goaltender wears a face mask.

CHAPTER 8 - PRACTICE DRILLS SPECIFICALLY FOR HOME

Playing hockey requires a high level of time-commitment. Hockey practices and games can fill up a player's weekly schedule quite easily! There are plenty of on-ice and off-ice weekly or even daily practices along with the hockey season's schedule of exhibition, regular season, tournament, and playoff games, which all require a high level of competitiveness! This list of practices and games is merely a fraction of the amount of commitments goaltenders will need to meet in order to successfully compete on a hockey team!

Goaltenders that spend the hockey season as described above will certainly *enjoy the game;* we have discovered over the years that this concept is just fine for most goaltenders. However, there is a *special cluster* of athletes that find it in their hearts to intrinsically want to excel as elite performers and ***win championships!***

This chapter has been specifically written for elite goaltenders (i.e., those that go the extra mile and strive to strengthen and perfect the skills required for effective goaltending). It takes a *special goaltender* to become a Champion; one that is willing to *sacrifice* many other pleasures of life!

There are two extremely valuable skill development drills that have been designed specifically for home use. These are drills that will separate elite goaltenders from recreational goaltenders.

The following two drills will bring the best out of you!

1. Racquet Ball Drill

Tighten the TRAPPER around your hand securely. Position yourself approximately ten feet away from a solid wall. Throw a racquet ball (because of its dynamic bouncing characteristics) so that it hits the wall about twelve inches above the floor. The ball will then bounce down towards the floor continuing back up simulating a puck rising from ice level.

React to the ball by focusing on it as it lands in the pocket of the TRAPPER. It is important to squeeze the ball at the precise moment it hits the pocket of the TRAPPER, otherwise it will bounce out in the form of a rebound!

The drill format includes catching **100 shots in a row** without dropping one. If the ball is dropped, then the goaltender must begin all over again until the drill is mastered.

How will it feel to be known as the goaltender with the fastest TRAPPER in the country? When this happens, we would like to emphasize that credit should be given to the Racquet Ball Drill and to your *sacrificial commitment* to be an Elite Goaltender and a Champion! *Elite* goaltenders also take advantage of the benefits of the Racquet Ball Drill by including it in their pre-game warm up ritual.

2. Shooting The Puck Drill

Puck-handling, for the modern day goaltender, has developed entirely into a specialized skill that truly separates elite goaltenders from recreational goaltenders.

The range of opportunities for goaltenders to obtain possession of the puck for his/her team by using the goal stick has become a key element of the game. Eager goaltenders will find that practicing their shot at home is the ONLY method of success in order to become an accomplished puck-handler.

IMPORTANT TEACHING MOMENT: *"Brent, I realize you catch with your right hand and that you normally shoot a hockey puck with a left-handed player stick. This is most uncommon … BUT, if you want to be an elite goaltender when you grow up, you will NEED to learn to shoot right-handed!"* /Coach Vic LeMire in a discussion with 9 year-old goaltender, Brent Bradford, in Osoyoos, BC at Vic's Hockey Schools.

"I remember that discussion like it was yesterday! I went home and practiced, practiced, and practiced until I could shoot right-handed accurately!" /Coach Brent Bradford

Drill #2 requires that a goaltender practices shooting a puck **100 times per day** (3 times per week). It is important for the goaltender to **wear both of his/her goaltender gloves** while performing this drill. A wrist shot is directed at a target that will be three feet above the ground.

STRIVE TO CREATE THE FOLLOWING CHALLENGE: If you hit the raised target *three times in a row* after the first 50 shots have been taken correctly, your daily lesson is complete! *Who can make it 53 shots?*

Coach Brent Bradford and Coach Vic LeMire's
OFFICIAL ELITE GOALTENDER HOME WORKOUT SCHEDULE

Racquet Ball Drill	3 days/week
Shooting the Puck Drill	3 days/week

CHAPTER 9 - TEAM PRACTICES

Goaltenders should give 100% effort during every single team practice. It is during team practices when goaltenders have opportunities to **master the skills** that are discussed throughout this book. A few tips for goaltenders to remember when it comes to team practices are listed below. Goaltenders must:

- be the first to step onto the ice prior to practice
- be the last to step off the ice following a practice
- maintain focus during every drill
- communicate effectively to teammates/coaches
- practice individual skills (e.g., puck-handling, skating)
- become educated with the coach's game plan
- become knowledgeable about all the different offensive attacks that coaches teach (e.g., 2-1-2)
- maintain game-like precision when it comes to following shooters during ODD- and EVEN-MAN OFFENSIVE ATTACKS
- be the first to arrive to the coach when the whistle blows
- be attentive to the Coaching Staff when they are describing a new drill

Goaltenders MUST ALWAYS begin each drill by being in the **Ready (SET) Position** while facing the puck at the origin of the drill? DO NOT be LAZY by simply standing at the completion spot of the drill!

WASTED TIME DOES NOT PAY OFF! Goaltenders that waste time during team practices by standing around, fooling around, or simply being unfocused are wasting both their time and their teammates' time. Goaltenders will not become fully *educated* if they waste time during team practices.

ATTENTION GOALTENDERS: *Elite* goaltenders *find time* during every team practice to work alone, or with their goaltender partners, on the most individualistic skills (e.g., sideways shuffles, butterfly slides, playing pucks behind the net, etc.), so that when it comes to game-time, the critical skills have been developed properly!

HOW DID YOU PERFORM DURING YOUR LAST TEAM PRACTICE?

PART THREE

DEVELOPING
GOALTENDER SKILLS

CHAPTER 10 - ESSENTIAL GOALTENDER SKILLS

Goaltenders require a rich amount of skills in order to keep up with offensive plays in and around the crease area. There is a plethora of basic skills that all young and inexperienced goaltenders must strive to master. There are also more advanced skills that all aspiring elite goaltenders MUST strive to grasp. Four key phases that relate to the development of the essential goaltender skills are as follows:

1. SKATING SKILLS. Goaltenders MUST strive to be the BEST skater on their teams. It is imperative that ALL goaltenders strive to enhance their skating abilities. They must be able to skate and move effectively forwards, backwards, laterally, and explosively in order to follow a puck that is being passed, stick-handled, or shot in and around the crease area. Goaltenders must also be able to skate quickly to the bench during a delayed penalty. They will need to win races to any loose pucks in order to prevent opposing players from getting to it first. Skating is extremely vital to a goaltender's success at *ALL* levels.

2. READY (SET) POSITION. The Ready (*SET*) Position is equally important to that of skating. Goaltenders must be fully prepared in a Ready (*SET*) Position to be able to react efficiently to offensive attacks. A goaltender that begins to react to a shot from the Ready (*SET*) Position will have much more success than a goaltender that reacts to a shot when standing in an upright position. The Ready (*SET*) Position provides goaltenders with the ability to perform the most essential goaltender tasks (e.g., explode out, load one leg, move into a high shot with the TRAPPER, skate quickly to the bench, move laterally, etc.).

IMPORTANT TEACHING POINT! You will notice, as you read the section above along with its more detailed explanation, that we have highlighted the word **(SET)** several times!

We wish to teach ALL goaltenders the IMPORTANCE of verbally, mentally, and/or even subconsciously making this **WORD - SET,** an essential skill that is included in your mobility game! Keep saying to yourself: **SET, SET, SET** with each movement as you follow the puck.

3. BALANCE, AGILITY, SPEED, and ANTICIPATION: All goaltenders must become acquainted with these significant terms. It is the goaltenders' balance, agility, speed, and anticipation that will separate their hockey success from others. Although the skating and Ready (SET) Position skills are crucial, if goaltenders do not possess balance, agility, speed, and anticipation when an offensive attack presents itself, they will not be able to handle it productively (e.g., a goal will most often be scored on a goaltender who loses his/her balance on a breakaway due to a lack of agility, foot speed, and/or anticipation).

4. FOLLOWING AND STOPPING THE PUCK. Generally, the most simplistic reason that a goaltender position exists is to keep the puck from entering the net ... PERIOD! Goaltenders must develop puck-stopping abilities and the high levels of tenacity and stubbornness that it takes to keep all pucks from crossing the goal line. They must be able to blend skating skills, the Ready (SET) Position, balance, agility, speed, and anticipation all together in order to stop pucks, defend plays effectively, and create plays productively.

RADICALLY UNCONVENTIONAL TECHNIQUES USED EFFECTIVELY: In order to compete successfully in a hockey game, you MUST strive to improve in all the areas mentioned in this chapter. It is the *EFFECTIVE* goaltender that can combine skating skills, the Ready (SET) Position, balance, agility, speed, and anticipation in order to fulfill all his/her responsibilities! Of course, we have observed, on more than one occasion, goaltenders stopping pucks with a minimal level of balance and absolutely no knowledge surrounding anticipation (e.g., a goaltender that falls onto his/her back on a breakaway, but makes the save because the goal stick went flying unintentionally into the air and stopped the puck, luckily!), but we want you to ask yourself, *How long do you believe this goaltender will be able to get away with not improving in these areas?*

KEY POINT: A goaltender that sprawls, dives, and flops in and around the crease area uncontrollably and without purpose will have difficulty progressing to *elite levels of hockey*. He/she may get away with these unintelligent goaltending techniques early in his/her minor hockey careers as the offensive players might not be high level shooters, passers, and play-makers; sooner or later, these shooters will become SNIPERS!

STANLEY CUP CHAMPIONSHIP EXAMPLES: Nevertheless, we have observed goaltenders applying radically unconventional lateral movement techniques during game action with success. Goaltenders, such as; **Tim Thomas** and **Dominic Hasek**, who *are filled with* control, purpose, and determination to do whatever it takes to stop the puck and WIN CHAMPIONSHIPS, are prime examples!

IMPORTANT NOTE: The mental and physical skills that all goaltenders should perfect may take a considerable amount of time to master. Coaches and parents/guardians must maintain an elevated level of attention to these important skills when working with goaltenders.

A Reminder from
Coach Brent Bradford and Coach Vic LeMire:

Goaltenders must be able to concentrate on the puck while maintaining a high level of focus on the offensive attack by reacting intelligently, aggressively, and confidently to the plays!

SKATING + *ELITE GOALTENDERS = REMARKABLE SKATERS!* Goaltenders that are able to reposition themselves quickly on the ice by using effective skating skills will have a greater chance of being successful. It is imperative that goaltenders are able to follow the puck as it moves around the crease area. In order for this to occur, goaltenders need to develop the basic skating skills (e.g., frontwards, backwards, and sideways skating).

IMPORTANT NOTE: The skating skills that are required for goaltenders are quite different from the skating skills that are required for forwards and defensemen. Goaltenders do not skate around the full ice surface during a game as players do, however, their movements require as much or more speed, balance, and control as any other players. Goaltenders can begin to work on other essential skills as soon as their skating skills reach *MASTERY LEVEL!*

CRITICAL POINT: Goaltenders MUST master the skill of skating! They MUST strive to be well-balanced, explosive, agile, and mobile while wearing proper fitting goaltender equipment.

Goaltenders must be one of the most effective skaters on the team. It is important to note that goaltender equipment weighs much more than equipment worn by forwards and defensemen. This fact, in itself, provides a major reason as to why goaltenders must practice skating skills each and every time they are on the ice.

A Reminder from
Coach Brent Bradford and Coach Vic LeMire:

Each time goaltenders participate in team practices, they must strive to master the skill of skating!
Goaltenders must practice goaltender-specific skating at least ten minutes per practice in order to enhance the following skills:
(1) balance, (2) explosiveness, (3) agility, and (4) mobility!

GOALTENDER-SPECIFIC SKATING

Goaltenders Should Perform Team Skating Drills! They should perform team skating drills with or without a puck (the same as forwards and defensemen). It is important to note that goaltenders will benefit greatly from performing team skating drills in the **READY (SET) POSITION.** This will enable them to become well-conditioned in order to employ proper skating techniques while remaining in the READY (SET) POSITION during game situations. This will also provide goaltenders with practice so they do not bob up and down; it will enhance their balance, explosiveness, agility, and mobility, which will be called upon during game situations.

IMPORTANT CONSIDERATION: Adjusting specific team skating drills is acceptable only when goaltenders cannot perform the drills due to the extra equipment being worn (e.g., shorten the skating distance required for goaltenders if they are slowing down the rest of the team, etc.).

ATTENTION: The unique skating skills listed below separate goaltenders from forwards and defensemen. These skating skills need to be *mastered*: Forwards and Backwards Skating in the READY (SET) POSITION, One-Foot and Two-Foot Stops, Sideways Shuffle, Sideways T-Glide, Mohawk Turn, Butterfly Crawl, and Butterfly Slide.

FORWARD/BACKWARD SKATING - *READY (SET) POSITION*

Goaltenders must possess the ability to move forwards and backwards while remaining in the proper **READY (SET) POSITION.** There are many goaltender-specific drills that can be implemented during practices to assist in the development of forwards and backwards skating. Goaltender-specific skating drills are most effective when they are shorter in distance (as close to game situations as possible) and provide goaltenders with opportunities to increase speed and enhance transition skills.

When goaltenders perform goaltender-specific skating drills, it is important to keep the skates as close to the ice as possible so that the READY (SET) POSITION is not disrupted, (e.g., upper body could lift up bringing the stick off the ice, five-hole could grow exceedingly large if the feet widen too much while moving in or out of the net).

HINT: Short strides allow goaltenders to keep the skates close to the ice while maintaining an effective READY (SET) POSITION. Repetitious drills are strategically more effective than long, drawn-out goaltender-specific skating drills.

DRILL EXAMPLE #1: Goaltenders will begin on the goal line in the proper READY (SET) POSITION. They will skate to the top of the face-off circle and stop using a One-Foot Stop (discussed in the section below - STOPPING). They will then begin to skate backwards in the proper READY (SET) POSITION to the initial starting point.

We would like to point out four important considerations to keep in mind when developing forward and backward skating in the proper READY (SET) POSITION.

1. Positioning. Goaltenders must become knowledgeable about where he/she is located in relation to the net at all times when moving in and out of the crease area in the proper READY (SET) POSITION.

IMPORTANT TIP: A very productive habit that *ALL* NHL goaltenders use is *tapping the post* with the shaft of their stick on one post and *tapping the post* with their Trapper on the other post. Elite goaltenders use this technique in order to stay familiar with where they are positioned in the net.

Learning to begin each **onslaught** in this same manner provides goaltenders with a familiar routine to begin the play. There are routines similar to this in ALL other sports (e.g., a golfer preparing to make a putt, a quarterback dropping back to make a pass, a tennis player preparing to begin a serve, a baseball player preparing to take a swing at a pitch)! All athletes begin with a familiar routine!

For goaltenders, touching the posts like this establishes the boundaries of their territory and lets them know where their posts and the center of their net are located! This will also enable goaltenders to face the play at all times by not getting turned sideways. Turning sideways would make them vulnerable to any potential shot.

2. Timing. Goaltenders must time their movements correctly. It is important for goaltenders to **NOT**:

- back up too quickly
- back up too far
- get caught too far out

Too Deep in Net	*Too Far Out of Net*

When goaltenders back into the crease area, it is vital for them to maintain the correct speed as an offensive player approaches. When an offensive player decides to slow down or speed up, the goaltender MUST match the player's speed.

EXAMPLE*:* A **breakaway situation** is an excellent example to solidify this point. Breakaways (see Chapter 24) will assist goaltenders in recognizing the importance of *holding their ground* and not backing up too quickly and/or too far.

3. Balance. Goaltenders must be well-balanced when moving in and out of the crease area. While moving in and out of the crease area, *elite* goaltenders are able to:

- distribute their weight properly

- position their arms productively

INEFFECTIVE   **EFFECTIVE**

- keep their sticks on the ice
- keep their upper bodies from bobbing up and down

IMPORTANT NOTE: Goaltenders that are unable to apply the four key concepts, mentioned above and depicted in the previous six pictures of *well-balanced goaltenders*, will not maintain a proper READY (SET) POSITION and will open up unnecessary holes.

4. Mobility. Goaltenders require outstanding mobility if they wish to reach *elite* status. Basic skating skills will not guide a goaltender to high levels of hockey. Goaltenders must possess the ability to reposition themselves all over the crease area smoothly with precision and control by using the edges of their skates.

COACHING TIP: Goaltenders must work with coaches that are willing to lead goaltender-specific skating drills that will enhance their forward and backward skating while maintaining a proper READY (SET) POSITION. Goaltenders will enhance mobility skills only when they decide to perform goaltender-specific skating drills each and every practice.

COMMON MISTAKE: It continues to be an extremely common error for goaltenders to lift up and swing their arms while skating forwards and backwards in the proper READY (SET) POSITION. This is the direct result for goaltenders' sticks lifting off the ice! This, in itself, is the reason why so many easy goals are scored; goaltenders' sticks must remain on the ice!

How Can Goaltenders Prevent This Situation? Goaltenders must constantly practice forwards and backwards skating while maintaining the proper READY (SET) POSITION to ensure that MASTERY LEVEL is achieved.

MOBILITY IN THE NET: The single most important skill that determines whether a hockey player plays in the NHL *or* is relegated to the minors is skating ability. This same skill-set, referred to as *Mobility*, is what goaltenders must develop to reach *elite* status!

Proper anticipation and many years of great goaltending experiences will certainly help goaltenders remain in front of an incoming shot, however, there is absolutely no greater replacement for goaltenders that have worked diligently on becoming *smooth and explosive warriors in the nets*!

There are three **mobility skills** that goaltenders MUST fully learn to develop. They are:

- quickness with their stops and starts
- possessing the ability to be EXPLOSIVE with their movements
- remaining very smooth and in control

ATTENTION GOALTENDERS: Your first-rate conditioning and superior athleticism will combine to provide you with the basis for becoming professionally quick around the crease. Very strong legs and totally ripped abdomen muscles are the beginnings of what will be required for you to move all that goaltending equipment around the crease.

Ultimately, goaltenders will find the most success when they are prepared in a **Ready (SET) Position**, as the shot is about to take place. Most often, however, goaltenders will have to **make the save while moving through the crease area** towards the puck.

IMPORTANT NOTE: It is critical that *elite* goaltenders maintain a strong stance as they move to follow passes in their own end. *ALL* professional goaltenders have learned the value of becoming SET, SET, SET using short, deliberate skating steps as they continually adjust their bodies to remain directly in front of the puck BEFORE it is shot toward them. *Educated* and *wise* goaltenders have learned how to keep their bodies centered on the puck while moving their heads to look around possible traffic screens in front of them.

Modern day goaltenders have learned to slide great distances across the crease area on the edges of their goal pads (e.g., **Cory Schneider, Marc-Andre Fleury,** and **Pekka Rinne** to name just a few). They can move back and forth remaining low to the ice as well as **EXPLODING OUT HARD** from the post in order to challenge shooters in front of the net during a *Pass-out* game situation (see Chapter 15). When scouting goaltenders, it is very easy to differentiate *elite* goaltenders from weaker goaltenders by simply analyzing their abilities to MOVE in and around the crease area!

Coach Brent Bradford & Coach Vic LeMire suggest:

If you want SUCCESS in the net ... learn to MOVE like the Legendary Goaltender and NHL Hall of Famer, Emile "The Cat" Francis!

STOPPING

Goaltenders need to be comfortable using two stopping methods:
(1) One-Foot Stop and (2) Two-Foot Stop.

1. One-Foot Stop: This is the most commonly used stopping method for goaltenders. It provides goaltenders with the ability to maintain the proper READY (SET) POSITION while transitioning from frontwards to backwards or vice versa. This method is used when a goaltender challenges a shooter explosively.

IMPORTANT NOTE: If a goaltender is required to begin skating backwards directly after a one-foot stop, the stopping foot should begin the first backwards C-Cut. This will enable the goaltender to stay well-balanced.

2. Two-Foot Stop: Goaltenders are often asked to *dart* to the bench during a delayed penalty and to *race* outside the crease area to retrieve a loose puck and play it to a teammate. It is during these game situations when goaltenders will not be required to be in the proper **READY (SET) POSITION**. These are the only game situations that provide goaltenders with opportunities to stop like a forward or defensemen.

LATERAL MOVEMENT

The major duty of goaltenders is to follow the puck as it moves around the crease area. As the puck enters the zone, it usually travels **east to west**, sideways. This forces goaltenders to develop effective lateral movement. To ensure that goaltenders cover as much net as possible when moving laterally, they MUST:

- keep the gloves in the proper position
- keep the stick from lifting off the ice
- maintain eye contact with the puck
- maintain good balance without bobbing up or down

We will discuss below five commonly used methods for moving laterally in and around the crease area: (1) Sideways Shuffle, (2) Sideways T-Glide, (3) Mohawk Turn, (4) Butterfly Crawl, and (5) Butterfly Slide.

There have been many different names for these four methods over the years. Also, there have been fragmented approaches stemming from these five basic methods (e.g., half-butterfly slide). These five basic lateral movement methods will be discussed in detail below.

IMPORTANT NOTE: When a goaltender's shoulders lift up, the stick automatically lifts off the ice; this can slow down lateral movement drastically and can open up unwanted holes! This is sometimes unpreventable as certain game situations call for goaltenders to get across faster than normal (e.g., due to a rare **defensive turnover**).

1. SIDEWAYS SHUFFLE. The Sideways Shuffle is a traditional movement that allows goaltenders to travel laterally around the crease area in order to follow the puck. It is accomplished by taking short sideways steps in the proper **READY (SET) POSITION** (a push-pull action with the skates). The lead skate pushes to the side as the weight is transferred onto that foot. The other skate, or *following skate*, is pulled along for the shuffle to be complete.

Goaltenders must remember to always maintain a proper **READY (SET) POSITION** in order to remain prepared to stop a shot. Goaltenders must strive to be centered on the puck while performing proper Sideways Shuffles; they should not back into the net while following a puck that is moving in front of the crease area.

The following is the list of important considerations to pay attention to when performing Sideways Shuffles during an offensive attack. A goaltender MUST:

1. keep the *leg pads* & *toes of the skates* always facing the puck (except in a Wrap-Around situation)
2. keep both skate blades parallel to each other
3. not allow the *skates* to be lifted off the ice
4. keep the stick blade on the ice covering the area between the leg pads
5. keep the gloves out and ready
6. not allow the upper body to bob up and down
7. maintain the proper READY (SET) POSITION throughout the series of sideways shuffles

SHOOTER KNOWLEDGE: The most effective place for a player to shoot from is directly in front of the net (i.e., slot area). However, ***elite*** goaltenders maintaining proper angles and positioning will cause offensive players to break to the sides; ***greatly decreasing their scoring chances***. The Sideways Shuffle is extremely effective in following this type of play; goaltenders need only to follow the basic steps mentioned above to follow the puck and keep it from entering the net.

IMPORTANT NOTE: Goaltenders can fulfill their duty of getting across the crease in short or long lateral steps; this depends on specific game situations (e.g., some game situations force goaltenders to cover a longer distance than others). The Sideways Shuffle should be practised consistently throughout the hockey season. There are many drills that can be implemented in practices to assist goaltenders in developing this necessary skating skill.

SHOOTING DRILL #1 - Line shooters up from *east to west* at the top of the face-off circles and have them shoot rapidly one after another.

IMPORTANT NOTE: Every shot MUST be no higher than the goaltender's waist area. **DO NOT SHOOT FOR THE TOP CORNERS** from this distance in practice!

Goaltenders will use the Sideways Shuffle proficiently while centering on each puck as they move from one player to the next player. It is important to ensure that goaltenders are not backing into the crease area as they move laterally; the shooters will have much more to shoot at if goaltenders retreat deep into the crease area.

2. SIDEWAYS T-GLIDE. The Sideways T-Glide must only be used when goaltenders are required to cover a large area when the puck is not in a danger zone (e.g., when opposing defensemen pass the puck to each other *east to west* - point to point - near the blue line).

The following is the list of important considerations to pay attention to when performing a Sideways T-Glide. In order to move laterally from left to right, a goaltender MUST:

1. turn the right skate blade so that it is at a 90 degree angle with the left skate blade
2. push off with the left skate blade which then drags behind allowing the right skate blade to extend out not allow the *skate blades* to be lifted off the ice
3. keep the blade of the stick on the ice covering the area between the leg pads
4. keep the gloves out and ready
5. not allow the upper body to bob up and down
6. return into the proper READY (SET) POSITION directly after each Sideways T-Glide

IMPORTANT NOTE: The Sideways T-Glide takes goaltenders out of their **READY (SET) POSITION** momentarily, which is an essential component in stopping pucks. The moment goaltenders turn the lead foot, the Sideways T-Glide has been fully committed. Goaltenders have a disadvantage if the puck is suddenly shot toward the net at this moment.

Why?
✓ The goaltender's legs are open as the lead skate blade is extended out sideways.
✓ The goaltender would be off balance as his/her weight is shifted onto the extended leg.
✓ The goaltender is momentarily vulnerable if the puck should suddenly head in the opposite direction.

3. MOHAWK TURN. Goaltenders **MUST** become comfortable on both the inside and outside edges of their skates. Specific game situations will call upon the goaltenders to perform *sharp MOHAWK TURNS* (e.g., when a goaltender has moved out to challenge a shooter who has pulled a fake shot and has pulled the puck back to try to go around the goaltender). A properly executed Mohawk Turn is performed when a goaltender remains in the proper **READY (SET) POSITION** as he/she is challenging out towards a perceived shot.

The inside skate must travel sharply on its outside edge; the outside skate must travel sharply on its inside edge. The stick blade must remain on the ice throughout the complete Mohawk Turn. It must be a sharp turn so that goaltenders can remain centered on the puck.

GOALTENDERS: The Mohawk Turn is a skating skill that uses forward momentum. The intention of this turn is to build momentum in order to:

- ✓ re-adjust the goaltender's positioning in relation to the puck suddenly moving east-to-west
- ✓ begin sideways shuffling
- ✓ back up into the crease area
- ✓ remain out and well-positioned in relation to the puck

The following is the list of important considerations to pay attention to when performing a Mohawk Turn. In order to cut a sharp turn to the left, a goaltender MUST:

1. move the left skate *forward* and *out* to the left followed closely by the right skate
2. lean over onto the outside edge of the left skate and onto the inside edge of the right skate
3. transfer weight onto the heels with bent knees
4. return from the weight forward position to a balanced position
5. keep the blade of the stick on the ice covering the area between the leg pads

IMPORTANT NOTE: In order to cut a sharp turn to the right, goaltenders must lead with the right skate and follow the steps listed above. A properly executed Mohawk Turn will carve a sharp/deep letter "C" into the ice using the heels of both skate blades.

A Mohawk Turn is an essential part of a goaltender's game. Goaltenders must strive to become comfortable on both the inside and outside edges in order to gain a sufficient amount of momentum when implementing this skill.

IMPORTANT NOTE: A Mohawk Turn will not be effective if the inside skate is travelling on its inside edge. Goaltenders will be unbalanced and unable to follow the play if this occurs.

4. BUTTERFLY CRAWL. The Butterfly Crawl is a movement that, resulting from new styles of leg pads (see Chapter 2), allows goaltenders to travel laterally around the crease area while on one knee in order to follow the puck.

| START POSITION | COMPLETION |

It is accomplished by taking short sideways steps stemming from a Butterfly position. The lead knee travels to the side as the weight is transferred onto that leg. The other leg's skate, or *following skate*, is pulled along for the crawl to be complete. That skate then digs into the ice near the leading leg's knee and drives another push to the side forcing the leading leg to travels sideways.

Goaltenders MUST always maintain a proper stick, blocker, and trapper position in order to be prepared to stop a shot. They must also strive to be centered on the puck while performing proper Butterfly Crawls;

goaltenders, that are following pucks moving **east to west** near the front of the crease, should not back into the net.

The following is the list of important considerations to pay attention to when performing Butterfly Crawls during an **offensive attack** near the crease area. Goaltenders MUST:

1. keep the leading leg pad flared out and always facing the puck in order to cover more net down low
2. keep the skate blade, which is following the leading leg pad, parallel to the direction being traveled
3. keep the stick blade on the ice covering the area between the leg pads
4. keep the Blocker and Trapper out and ready
5. not allow the upper body to bob up and down

SHOOTER KNOWLEDGE: When a shooter observes that a goaltender is following the puck in the Butterfly Crawl position, he/she may decide to pull the puck back and shoot for the top portion of the net. If this occurs and there is a direct line from the puck into the net, the goaltender MUST get back up in order to protect the upper part of the net!

ATTENTION GOALTENDERS: We see too many goaltenders not understanding when to get up out of a Butterfly Crawl position and letting easy goals in because they are down on the ice. The Butterfly Crawl technique MUST only be used to follow the puck when it is in tight to the crease area and when the puck does not have a direct line into the top portion of the net! It is not a technique that should be used when a puck is in the slot area or further out. This technique MUST be used only when the puck is in tight! Ask yourselves: **When I am in the Butterfly Crawl position, can the puck see a direct line into the net over my shoulders?** If the answer is YES...GET UP!

The Butterfly Crawl should be practiced consistently throughout the hockey season at all levels. There are many drills that can be implemented in team practices to help goaltenders develop this necessary skating skill.

SHOOTING DRILL #1: Line shooters up from **east to west** just outside the top of the crease area. Have the shooters travel with a puck, one at a time, across the top of the crease area (far enough out so the goaltender cannot poke the puck away). The goaltender will use the Butterfly Crawl proficiently while centering on the puck as the player is traveling **east to west** in front of him/her.

It is important to make sure the goaltender is not backing into the crease area as he/she moves laterally; the shooters will have much more to shoot at if the goaltender retreats deep into the crease area. When the shooter arrives at the other side of the net, he/she will shoot high or low. The next shooter will travel in the opposite direction which will allow the goaltender to practice the Butterfly Crawl in both directions.

When the goaltender begins to master this drill, allow the shooters to change direction throughout their travels. This will force the goaltender to transfer weight, dig in with the opposite skate, and become effective at changing directions!

5. BUTTERFLY SLIDE - What A Great Save! When the puck is passed across the top of the crease area from one opposing player to another in an attempt to score on an empty net (forcing goaltenders to get across quickly), an effective save selection to implement is the productive Butterfly Slide. The Butterfly Slide recently replaced the traditional Pad Stack as it provides goaltenders with a more effective form of puck control, body control, and post-save recovery.

THE GLOVE MUST BE OPEN ... AND FACING THE PUCK!

In order to move across smoothly from a goaltender's Blocker side to the Trapper side ... and in time for the shot, the following are some tips for goaltenders to grasp. Goaltenders MUST:

1. quickly drive the lead leg's knee down to the ice so that the skate blade lifts off the ice and a slide can occur with the leading pad
2. turn the head quickly to figure out (in a millisecond) where the player receiving the puck is located in relation to the crease
3. push EXPLOSIVELY with the outside leg so that a powerful slide across the crease can occur
4. keep the Trapper up, out, and open facing where the puck is potentially going to be shot from
5. lead with the stick blade on the ice so that it is able to cover the area between the legs

ATTENTION GOALTENDERS: The pushing leg MUST spring into action after its initial push and slam together with its opposite knee to form a solid Butterfly in the correct spot to make the save.

STICK ON THE ICE ... NO HOLES THROUGH THE MIDDLE ...
A SOLID BUTTERFLY SAVE IS IMMINENT!

WHAT SHOULD THIS GOALTENDER
DO WITH THE PUCK AFTER THE SAVE?

In order to move across smoothly from a goaltender's Trapper side to the Blocker side ... and in time for the shot, the following are some tips for goaltenders to follow. Goaltenders MUST:

1. quickly drive the lead leg's knee down to the ice so that the skate blade lifts off the ice and a slide can occur with the leading pad
2. turn the head quickly to figure out (in a millisecond) where the player receiving the puck is located in relation to the crease
3. push EXPLOSIVELY with the outside leg so that a powerful slide across the crease can occur

Goaltenders ... what does the OUTSIDE LEG refer to?

4. lead with the stick blade on the ice so that it is able to cover the area between the legs
5. keep the Trapper up, out, and open facing where the puck is potentially going to be shot from

ATTENTION GOALTENDERS: The pushing leg MUST spring into action after its initial push and slam together with its opposite knee to form a solid Butterfly in the correct spot to make the save.

The Butterfly Slide can be observed many times during a game in high level hockey.

Elite and educated goaltenders, after mastering this skill, are able to travel across the crease smoothly using a Butterfly Slide, make the save, and deal with any potential rebounds by:

1. covering the puck up
2. sending the puck to the corner as it deflects effectively off of the goaltender equipment (e.g., pads, stick, blocker, upper body)
3. catching the puck and taking a whistle (this type of save usually ends up with a loud cheer from the crowd!)

Goaltenders that are aiming to reach *elite* levels of hockey MUST maintain a high level of focus in order to MASTER the Butterfly Slide.

ATTENTION GOALTENDERS: It is imperative that you continue to develop your smoothness, explosiveness, and tightness with this skill.

You should practice the Butterfly Slide with some players whenever you have time so that during a game, you can steal some sure goals and ... MAKE THIS SKILL LOOK EASY!

BUTTERFLY SLIDE PRACTICE DRILL #1 - Line a few pucks on the face-off dots in the goaltender's end. Have one player on the face-off dot pass one puck at a time to another player that is standing near the top of the crease on the opposite side ready to receive the pass and shoot high or low in a quick manner.

As the goaltender makes his/her way across the crease using the Butterfly Slide, he/she MUST focus on two extremely important occurrences that will be required from them:

1. making the initial save
2. deciding what to do with the puck after the initial save (e.g., cover it, send it to the corner, etc.)

IMPORTANT NOTE: Most goaltenders can stop pucks, elite goaltenders know what they are going to do with the puck prior to stopping it!

READY (*SET*) POSITIONS - STANCES

Goaltender *stances* have morphed into a wide variety of positional poses throughout the game of hockey's glorious history!

TAKE A MOMENT: We MUST first honour the pioneers of the position and admire the ***maskless men of iron!*** With stitches like a road map covering the faces of these brave souls, they began the goaltending position by making most of their saves using a ***stand up stance*** entirely.

A SALUTE TO LEGENDARY GOALTENDERS: Plante, Worsley, and Crozier: (In 1964, acrobatic goaltender, **Roger Crozier** entered the NHL introducing the advent of the ***Butterfly Goaltender***. He was awarded the ***Calder Memorial Trophy*** as the league's *Top Rookie*. He also became the first player to win the ***Conn Smythe Trophy (Playoff MVP)*** in a losing effort. His team lost to the Montreal Canadiens in the Stanley Cup Finals that season!

BUTTERFLY STANCE. More and more goaltenders began to use the *Butterfly Style* consistently during game situations after observing the success of Roger Crozier in 1964. It is simple to point out that in today's game the value of protecting ALL of the lower ice-level shots with a massive butterfly save is an effective strategy to implement!

GOALTENDERS: The *Butterfly Save* begins with a very wide leg spread while remaining standing up on your feet. With both knees pressing against each other, you are now positioned to cover the outer edges of the goal net (both posts) with the toes!

As the shot is about to take place, you must quickly **EXPLODE** your knees very hard and deliberately down to the ice *BEFORE the puck arrives.* This explosive action closes the 5-hole with the blade of the goal stick pressing firmly against the ice between the legs.

The *Trapper* must also remain **WIDE OPEN** at the side of the goaltender just above the leg pad. Both elbows of the goaltender must also be held tight to the body forming a very solid and wide *butterfly stance*.

IMPORTANT NOTE: The *Butterfly Stance* is not as effective if the goaltender is positioned **DEEP** in the net. *For extreme success, the Butterfly Stance is most effective when the goaltender is very aggressive and is positioned well out (challenging above the crease)!*

SOLID STANCE. The value of the *Solid Stance* is not forgotten in the modern game. It is *the save of choice* on a *deep, severe angle shot* which is described in detail in Chapter 23.

EFFECTIVE SAVE SELECTION

CHAPTER 11 - USING THE STICK

An extremely important part of a goaltender's arsenal is the use of the stick (aka *"The Lumber"*). It is often observed that **fans go wild** whenever a goaltender loses his/her stick during a play! It is very common to think that a goaltender is vulnerable when the stick is lying on the ice. *How can a goaltender protect the five-hole in a butterfly position, move a rebound to the soft corner, or direct a puck that is shot hard along the ice from the point?* The answer lies in each specific goaltender's level of experience. Some goaltenders are able to make effective saves without the stick. However, it is much more difficult to make a key save without **the lumber**. Every goaltender must learn how to hold onto the stick during **ALL** game situations so that they are fully prepared to make productive saves and plays.

Elite goaltenders are able to use the stick as both an offensive and defensive goaltending tool. The key purposes of this tool are to:

1. Stop the Puck
2. Cover (pull in) the Puck
3. Clear the Puck
4. Direct the Puck
5. Poke Check the Puck/Player
6. Pass the Puck
7. Shoot the Puck
8. Play the Puck Shot Around the Boards
9. Race for the Puck

Goaltenders that have mastered the use of the stick will have an easier time stopping, controlling, and handling the puck than goaltenders that have not.

CONTROLLING REBOUNDS

Players usually look for rebounds when pucks are shot hard along the ice. Handling potential rebounds is an important skill that requires the use of the stick. When a puck is shot along the ice toward the net, it is imperative for the goaltender to decide what he/she will do with the puck **BEFORE** it makes contact with the stick. Effective methods of handling (controlling) rebounds will be discussed below.

IMPORTANT NOTE: Elite goaltenders will survey the positioning of **ALL** the players involved in the play before the shot arrives. This will enable them to decide upon the most intelligent choice that can be made with a potential rebound. Questions that need to be addressed *in milliseconds* for this situation are:

✓ *Where is the BEST place for the rebound to go?*
✓ *Is deflecting the puck to the safe corner zones better than deflecting the puck out of play into the stands?*

Did You Know ...

The first NHL goaltender to score a goal by shooting the puck into the opposing net was Philadelphia's Ron Hextall. He scored into an empty net against the Boston Bruins after the team pulled their goaltender in the final minute of the game. He scored his second goal in the Stanley Cup Playoffs ... which team did he score a playoff goal against?

1. Stopping The Puck

If the goaltender wishes to have the puck stop right in front of him/her, he/she must ensure that the stick blade is held straight up and is positioned a few inches in front of the toes (the puck will bounce off quickly and head back into the danger zone if the stick is held tightly against the toes).

Modified Method: Goaltenders can also place their Trapper behind the stick blade if time permits. This technique will also help stop the puck without letting out any rebounds.

IMPORTANT DECISION-MAKING TIME: Once a goaltender has stopped the puck effectively and has controlled any potential rebounds, he/she is required to make the next important decision that will involve the stick (e.g., cover, clear, pass, or shoot the puck).

2. Covering The Puck

After the goaltender has stopped a puck shot hard along the ice and controlled any potential rebounds, he/she may recognize that covering the puck and forcing a stoppage in play is the most productive decision for his/her team's well-being. For example:

✓ *Does your team need a line change? This will help your coach match line combinations when playing at home thereby taking advantage of last change privileges (e.g., knowing you want your BEST defense combination playing against their TOP line).*
✓ *Slowing the game down when the opposition is playing with high intensity and fore-checking extremely hard.*
✓ *When a teammate loses his/her stick.*
✓ *When killing a penalty - especially when playing two men short.*

When covering the puck with the Trapper, it is imperative to protect the Trapper with the stick. If the stick is not protecting the Trapper, the opposition's players may knock the puck free allowing an unwanted rebound opportunity. Covering your Trapper with your stick also helps to protect the fingers of your Trapper hand.

3. Clearing The Puck

Covering the puck is not always the most productive play after a goaltender has stopped and controlled it. Clearing the puck into a safe zone (e.g., the soft corner) may be a more desirable decision when a specific game situation presents itself. For example:

✓ *Help to start a quick breakout potentially trapping one or two aggressive fore-checkers.*
✓ *Wanting to kill the last few seconds of a period or a game without a whistle stopping the play.*

If it is important to not get a face-off in the defensive zone, a goaltender should clear the puck with the stick to the corner with a one-handed backhand or forehand pass.

Did You Know …

In 1928-29, George Hainsworth of the Montreal Canadiens played 44 games and recorded an astounding 22 shutouts.

---

4. Directing The Puck

Some specific game situations force goaltenders to direct pucks that have been shot hard along the ice rather than stopping it. Directing a puck with the stick is an extremely important skill to master. Keeping the stick blade along the ice allows goaltenders to direct pucks to either corner without having to worry about any unwanted rebounds occurring in front of them.

ATTENTION GOALTENDERS: *Elite goaltenders* already know what they are going to do with a puck that is shot hard along the ice prior to it even arriving. *Are you going to be prepared to make these important decisions when a puck is shot hard along the ice (e.g., stop, cover, clear, direct the puck)?*

Did You Know ...

Goaltending Specialist and Pioneer, Vic LeMire, played goal in Junior A, Major Junior, Canadian University, and NCAA hockey. If you require pertinent information about these various leagues, he is the person to chat with; after all, he has playing experience in all four leagues.

5. Poke Checking The Puck/Player: Secret Weapon

There are many **BATTLES** that goaltenders are forced to engage in throughout a hockey game. Chapter 20 discusses **Rebounds** and **Rebound Control**. It is imperative for goaltenders at all levels to understand fully that *losing the BATTLE* on *Rebounds* will most assuredly conclude with a negative outcome...a *GOAL AGAINST*!

Losing a different type of BATTLE on the *Goaltender's ICE* will be explained in detail throughout the next few pages. The designated patch *of extremely valuable, high rent frozen real estate,* known as the Goaltender's Crease, is MORE than just a painted area on the ice. It is much more than that! The actual goaltender's crease includes several feet of *goaltender territory* in front of and all around the outside of the painted area. A goaltender that relinquishes this sub-zero battlefield to the opposition does so with the risk of great peril to his/her team!

ATTENTION GOALTENDERS: A passive, non-aggressive goaltender in this situation becomes nothing more than a *spectator on blades*! We would like to emphasize loudly - *The most effective position for a goaltender with a passive, non-aggressive attitude is on the bench opening and closing the gate!*

THIS IS NOT GOING TO BE YOU! Goaltenders who crave to compete at an elite level must have a *SECRET WEAPON* in their goaltender arsenal.

WHAT IS THE SECRET WEAPON?

The Goaltender's Secret Weapon: A Poke Check is a chapter in this book that every elite goaltender must commit to memory verbatim! We will teach all the physical techniques, all the game situations, and all the mental on-ice chess scenarios that need to be understood in order to outright *OWN* the goaltenders' **valuable property on the ice**! There are several reputations a goaltender should strive to establish in hockey.

ONE DESIRABLE REPUTATION: Being recognized as a strong, aggressive goaltender that battles intensely all around the net is a *gold mine* of a reputation to obtain!

The Poke Check - *Physical Aspects:* There are important physical movements that are required for a successful poke check. All of the movements MUST be combined together as **one** **EXPLOSIVE SAVE PACKAGE!** This entire *save package* must be executed in a split second! It MUST be **practised over and over and over again** until it becomes **lightening quick!**

The Goal Of The Poke Check: To surprise a player quickly – *snake-like*!

Remember: Do not let anyone handle the puck near your valuable property on the ice without letting them know it is YOUR ICE!

GOALTENDER STATEMENT:

This is my ice and I would like to introduce you to my...SECRET WEAPON! BOOM!

IMPORTANT PHYSICAL MOVEMENTS OF THE POKE CHECK

1. Begin low in your crouch as you are positioned out at the **Top of the Goal Crease!**
2. Use a very quick and **explosive** sliding of your hand **ALL** the way up to the knob of the goal stick.

3. Shift your weight to your foot that is on your Blocker side, focusing on digging into the ice with the toe of your blade. This **loads your leg** preparing for an **explosive attack**!

4. Drive your entire body **outstretched fully** with an **explosive slide**!

ATTENTION GOALTENDERS: The most effective strategy is to **intercept the path** of all three of these objects. They are:

   i. The Puck
  ii. The Player's Stick Blade
 iii. The Player's Skates

TEACHING POINT #1 - The *direction* that a goaltender MUST aim the explosive poke check and his/her explosive, fully outstretched body slide is ... <u>AHEAD</u> of the path of the travelling puck!

A goaltender should never aim toward the puck when attempting a poke check. If a goaltender were to aim toward the puck, the puck will NOT be there anymore when the goal stick finally arrives! The result will almost certainly become a GOAL AGAINST!

Grab Stick Here

TEACHING POINT #2 - It is **equally important** to EXPLODE UP onto your feet, as quickly as you went down, to execute a successful poke check! A loose puck will most likely be out there somewhere in front of the net. It is the goaltender's responsibility to find the loose puck and to get centered on it once again.

The Poke Check - *Game Situations*: It is important to recognize that a goaltender's catching hand (i.e., right or left) will impact his/her poke checking decisions.

Goaltenders that *catch with their **left hand*** should only attempt to **poke check left-handed shooters** infringing on their valuable property!

Conversely, goaltenders that *catch with their **right hand*** should only attempt to **poke check right-handed shooters** infringing on their valuable property!

This is structurally an important teaching/learning point for all goaltenders to commit to memory. The mechanics of the poke check dictate that true success will most often occur when abiding entirely by this lesson!

KEY POINT: *A VARIATION TO BE CONSIDERED* - It is important to recognize that a different form of a poke check, **using a wide, sweeping motion**, may be effective from time to time against right-handed shooters attacking goaltenders that catch with the left hand. This is not, however, a recommended *save selection* for this game situation! Using a *Paddle-Down Save* is recommended in this situation for a goaltender to be successful against a right-handed shooter.

The three game situations that are truly poke check candidates are:

✓ *A player, skating out of the corner, trying to drive entirely across the front of the net with the puck.*
✓ *A player, cutting in from the wing, trying to drive totally across the front of the net with the puck.*
✓ *A player on a breakaway, or in a shoot-out (if the situation presents itself properly, which can be set up strategically by the goaltender – (see Chapter 25).*

In order to use the **Secret Weapon** (i.e., the **Poke Check**) successfully, a goaltender *MUST trick the shooter* into believing he/she can skate all the way around him/her. Thus, a goaltender can give the shooter a quick *FAKE* with a slight move to the short side by actually loading up his/her leg for a poke check slide. This move will force the shooter to decide to go around the goaltender.

The goaltender is always in charge!
Goaltenders ... Force the shooter to do what <u>YOU</u> want!

The Poke Check - *Mental Preparation:* Coach Brent Bradford and Coach Vic LeMire are highly aware of the advantages a goaltender gains when he/she takes full control of the play around the goal crease!

***A Goaltender in CHARGE
is a goaltender that plays LARGE!***

On-Ice Chess Scenario*:** Consider what a shooter would do if a goaltender begins to make a move (fake) to poke check, too early (e.g., a head fake or a short step away from the shooter)? ***Correct! The shooter will STOP his/her movement from going entirely across the top of the goal crease. Subsequently, he/she will try to score on the short side.

TIME TO THINK: So, in this situation, did the shooter do what he/she wanted to do, OR, did the shooter do what the ***goaltender forced the shooter to do***? ***YES! The goaltender is in charge and forced the play to occur!*** A *FAKE* Poke Check is just as valuable as a *REAL* Poke Check.

Practising the poke check at home will greatly improve its effectiveness. Goaltenders MUST continue to work on the explosiveness and the directional aspects of the Poke Check and always be prepared to state:

"HEY ... ALL YOU OPPOSING SHOOTERS ...

*WHEN YOU COME NEAR MY
FROZEN REAL ESTATE WITH THE PUCK ...*

WATCH OUT FOR MY SECRET WEAPON: MY POKE CHECK!"

<u>REMEMBER GOALTENDERS</u>

MAKE IT SNAKE-LIKE! LIGHTNING QUICK!

PLAYING PUCKS

Playing pucks is a required skill for **elite** *goaltenders*. We have observed goaltenders playing pucks effectively as young as eight years old. This section will outline proper techniques for passing pucks, shooting pucks, playing pucks shot around the boards, and racing for pucks. All of these skills require proper usage of the *stick*.

6. Passing The Puck

There are many opportunities during a game when it is best for a goaltender to become involved and pass the puck safely.

A goaltender that is capable of passing pucks effectively …
will be an asset to any team!

ATTENTION GOALTENDERS: Coaches are able to implement new team strategies when they recognize that their goaltender possesses the ability to pass the puck productively during a play.

Passing the puck can refer to the following:

✓ *moving the puck into the soft corner*
✓ *hitting a winger with the puck on the hash-marks and boards*
✓ *passing to a teammate that has left the penalty box out past the blue line, and much more*

Whether a goaltender is passing pucks short or long distances, it is imperative to follow a few simple guidelines.

IMPORTANT NOTE: As we explain in detail a variety of techniques for passing the puck, it is important to remember that goaltenders **MUST ALWAYS** make the **EASY PLAY** when handling the puck. Forcing a pass through opposing players **WILL** create unwanted problems (e.g., the pass could be intercepted by an opposing player).

SHORT DISTANCE PASSES IN YOUR OWN END: The stick blade should be *kept low* during the follow through so the pass remains low and quick *along the ice.*

LONG DISTANCE PASSES INTO THE NEUTRAL ZONE: The stick blade should be *raised up* during the follow through so the pass becomes a hard, line drive pass in the air, ***off the ice.***

Two-Handed Forehand Flip Pass: To execute this pass most productively, a goaltender MUST pay attention to the following:

1. Grasp the end of the stick with the Blocker hand and grasp the stick near the top of the shaft with the Trapper. **IMPORTANT NOTE:** The Trapper should be turned over.

2. The Trapper should be able to push the stick down toward the ice (applying pressure for a quick snap).

3. In order to flip the puck into the air, the puck should begin on the front-side heel of the stick blade; it should roll off the front-side toe of the stick blade.

4. The stick blade should be raised up during the follow through. The puck should flip off of the toe of the stick blade.

Two-Handed Backhand Flip Pass: To execute this pass most productively, goaltenders MUST pay attention to the following:

1. Grasp the end of the stick with the Blocker hand and grasp the stick near the top of the shaft with the Trapper. **IMPORTANT NOTE:** The Trapper should be turned over.

2. In order to flip the puck into the air, the puck should begin on the back-side heel of the stick blade; it should roll off the back-side mid-point of the stick blade.
3. The stick blade should be raised up during the follow through. The puck should flip off of the mid-point of the stick blade.

One-Handed Backhand Flip Pass: To execute this pass most productively, a goaltender MUST pay attention to the following:

1. Turn his/her body sideways toward the target (the Trapper arm should be the closest body part to the target).
2. Hold the stick exactly the same as when he/she is in the READY (SET) POSITION.
3. Control the puck and drag it back across his/her body and set it on the back-side heel of the stick blade.

4. Sweep the puck (i.e., a pulling action) back across the front of his/her body quickly and let the puck roll off the back-side mid-point of the stick blade.
5. In order to flip the puck into the air, the puck should begin on the back-side heel of the stick blade; it should roll off the back-side mid-point of the stick blade.
6. The stick blade should be raised up during the follow through. The puck should flip off of the mid-point of the stick blade.

One-Handed Forehand Pass. *(Used for short passes only)*. To execute this pass most productively, a goaltender MUST pay attention to the following:

1. Turn his/her body sideways toward the target (the Blocker arm should be the closest body part to the target).
2. Hold the stick exactly the same as when he/she is in the READY (SET) POSITION.
3. Control the puck and set it on the front-side mid-point of the stick blade.

4. Sweep the puck (i.e., a pushing action) quickly and let the puck roll off the front-side toe of the stick blade.
5. Follow through with the Blocker.

One-Handed Backhand Pass: To execute this pass most productively, a goaltender MUST pay attention to the following:

1. Turn his/her body sideways toward the target (the Trapper arm should be the closest body part to the target).
2. Hold the stick exactly the same as when his/her is in the READY (SET) POSITION.
3. Control the puck and drag it back across his/her body and set it on the back-side heel of the stick blade.
4. Sweep the puck (i.e., a pulling action) back across the front of his/her body quickly and let the puck roll off the back-side mid-point of the stick blade.
5. Follow through with the Blocker.

Two-Handed Backhand Pass: To execute this pass most productively, a goaltender MUST pay attention to the following:

1. Grasp the end of the stick with the Blocker hand.
2. Grasp the stick near the top of the shaft with the Trapper. **IMPORTANT NOTE:** The Trapper should be turned over.
3. The Trapper should be able to help sweep the puck along the ice.
4. The puck should begin on the back-side heel of the stick blade; it should roll off the back-side mid-point of the stick blade.
5. The stick blade should be kept low during the follow through so the pass remains low and quick along the ice.

IMPORTANT NOTE: Every goaltender that aspires to reach high levels of hockey MUST strive to increase his/her passing skills. Coaches should promote the importance of this skill by implementing a rich amount of opportunities for goaltenders to pass pucks in game-like situations during practices. If goaltenders are expected to be effective puck-handlers, they NEED ample practice time with teammates.

Team Practice Drill - *Controlling Dump-Ins*: Have the goaltender retrieve a common game-like dump-in (e.g., flipped in, shot in quickly on net or around the boards, etc.) by controlling the puck. Once the puck is under control, the goaltender has several options with the puck. He/she can:

➢ pass it to a teammate on the boards
➢ pass it outside the blue line
➢ set it up **behind the net** for a smooth transfer to a teammate

The player who receives the pass can skate hard with the puck to the other end of the ice for a shot on net. This drill can occur from both ends involving both goaltenders.

7. Shooting The Puck

Goaltenders that possess the ability to shoot a puck accurately and with enough force to be effective are assets to any team! Shooting a puck during game action can look similar to passing a puck with one small difference. When shooting a puck, goaltenders may not always have an intended receiver. For instance, shooting a puck hard along the glass may be an attempt to simply clear the zone and let the two teams fight for the puck in the neutral zone. Another common situation when *elite* goaltenders shoot the puck productively is when they decide to fire the puck over the players' heads in order to send it to the other end of the ice. The key components of shooting a puck effectively can be broken down into the same parts as the **Two-Handed Forehand Pass**.

8. Playing Pucks Shot Around The Boards

Stopping and playing pucks behind the net is an essential skill that **ALL** goaltenders should strive to enhance. Stopping a puck that is shot around the boards is a relatively simple concept. There are two proven techniques that will be covered in this section.

Proven Technique #1 - TRAPPER SIDE

Shooting Position: When a puck is shot hard along the boards on a goaltender's Trapper side, the goaltender must skate to the back boards from the same side of the net with explosive power.

Once the goaltender arrives near the boards behind the net, he/she will get into the **Two-Handed Forward Pass** position with the toe of the stick blade touching the boards. When the goaltender is in this position with control of the puck, he/she MUST make a productive and extremely quick decision with the puck (e.g., shoot, pass, flip, set, reverse the puck, etc.).

Proven Modified Technique #2 - TRAPPER SIDE

Ready (SET) Position: When a puck is shot hard along the boards on a goaltender's Trapper side, the goaltender must skate to the back boards from the same side of the net with explosive power. Once the goaltender arrives near the boards behind the net, he/she will get in the Ready (SET) Position with the toe of the stick blade touching the boards while the closest leg pad is tight to the boards. With this technique, it is important to quickly get into the passing/shooting position after the puck is stopped, unless the aim is to simply set it for a defenseman.

When the goaltender is in this position with control of the puck, he/she MUST make a productive and extremely quick decision with the puck (e.g., shoot, pass, flip, set, reverse the puck, etc.).

Proven Technique #1 - BLOCKER SIDE

Shooting Position: When a puck is shot hard along the boards on a goaltender's Blocker side, the goaltender must skate to the back boards from the same side of the net with his/her back now facing the puck and with his/her head on a swivel waiting for the puck. Once the goaltender arrives near the boards behind the net, he/she will get in the **Two-Handed Backhand Pass** position with the toe of the stick blade touching the boards.

When the goaltender is in this position with control of the puck, he/she MUST make a productive and extremely quick decision with the puck (e.g., shoot, pass, flip, set, reverse the puck, etc.).

Proven Modified Technique #2 - BLOCKER SIDE

Ready (SET) Position: When a puck is shot hard along the boards on a goaltender's Blocker side, the goaltender must skate to the back boards from the same side of the net with explosive power stopping with a one-foot stop prior to arriving at the boards and then reaching to the boards with one hand on the stick in the one-hand backhand formation.

It is important to quickly get into the passing/shooting position after the puck is stopped, unless the aim is to simply set it for a defenseman.

When the goaltender is in this position with control of the puck, he/she MUST make a productive and extremely quick decision with the puck (e.g., shoot with a **One-Handed Backhand** or pivot and shoot a **Two-Handed Forehand** around the net, pass, flip, set, reverse the puck, etc.).

Ineffective Technique: We have observed goaltenders over the past few years carry out an ineffective technique for stopping pucks shot around the boards. This unproductive technique has the goaltenders turning their backsides to the boards forcing the puck to be stopped by the outside of the foot/skate.

The dangers of this ineffective technique are:

✓ it will cause a goaltender to lose control of the puck as it deflects off his/her skate dangerously out to the front of the open net
✓ it prevents goaltenders from moving the puck quickly as he/she becomes stuck out of position during an aggressive fore-check (the puck is pinned against the boards by the skate preventing the goaltender from moving the puck should an aggressive fore-check present itself)

9. Racing For Pucks

ELITE goaltenders are aggressive! **ELITE** goaltenders are able to race for loose pucks due to their high level of skating skills and confidence. Deciding to race for loose pucks is a skill that can be very beneficial for a goaltender that wishes to reach high levels of hockey! However, racing for loose pucks can get a goaltender in HUGE trouble, if two areas are not addressed;

✓ Skating
✓ Hesitation

Skating: A goaltender that wishes to explode outside of the crease area to race for a loose puck MUST be an excellent skater. Once a goaltender decides to race for a loose puck, he/she must skate **ALL OUT** and must decide what will be done with the puck **BEFORE** the race is won (e.g., cover it, clear it, shoot it, etc.).

Hesitation: Once a goaltender decides to race for a loose puck, **the decision needs to be final!** If a goaltender decides to go for it, then he/she decides to hang back, then he/she decides to go for it again...*it is WAY too late!*

Racing for loose pucks, and winning the race, will gain a goaltender a lot of praise from coaches and teammates. Also, *elite* goaltenders that are effective at winning races for loose pucks are sending the correct messages to professional scouts sitting in the stands!

What Messages Are You Sending To Scouts? A goaltender that wins races for loose pucks demonstrates an aggressive, confident attitude with an exceedingly high level of understanding toward the *Game of Hockey!*

SUMMARIZING POINT: It is essential that goaltenders at ALL levels are provided with a rich amount of opportunities to practice stopping, covering, clearing, directing, passing, shooting, and playing pucks, as well as racing for loose pucks, during team practices. They will become more fully prepared for actual game situations if they execute these skills successfully during practices.

Did You Know ...

The most famous son from Sandon, BC (i.e., one of BC's most famous former mining towns), Cecil "Tiny" Thompson, who was born in 1905, won four Vezina Trophies during his 12-year NHL career and helped the Boston Bruins win its first Stanley Cup in 1929. In 1932-33, he led the NHL with a career-high 11 shutouts. Thompson, a First Team All-Star, became the very first goaltender to earn an assist in the NHL. He was elected to the Hockey Hall of Fame in 1959.

CHAPTER 12 - USING THE TRAPPER

The Trapper can be the most impactful piece of equipment that goaltenders wear. It can provide goaltenders with an excellent tool during game action when it is used productively. Catching shots should be the first choice by goaltenders. When they catch pucks, many options become available to them, such as:

➢ waiting for a whistle
➢ shooting the puck down the ice
➢ moving the puck to the corner
➢ making a pass to a teammate

IMPORTANT NOTE: These four basic options are available only because the puck was initially caught by the goaltender and because there was no rebound from the initial shot.

Goaltenders become in charge of the play once they catch the puck!

Goaltenders MUST strive to catch all pucks that are off the ice except when they are required to dive or are taken out of position. If a shot, which is headed toward the Blocker side is *not too hard,* it is not a bad idea to reach over to catch the puck (be attentive to the term *too hard* when choosing this strategy). If the puck is shot *too hard* to reach over in time, then make the stop simply with the Blocker.

ATTENTION GOALTENDERS: You will require quick reflexes and a proper **Ready (SET) Position** in order to catch pucks. Your Trapper must be open toward the puck. As the puck enters the Trapper, squeeze it! You do not want to have a puck fall out in front of you allowing an unwanted rebound to occur.

The Trapper should be in sight at all times. It should be out in front a bit, not uncomfortably close to the body. This allows for more freedom of movement and for goaltenders to watch the puck easily as it enters the Trapper.

IMPORTANT MODIFICATION: Elite goaltenders are able to understand when to modify the Trapper position when faced with two specific game situations (e.g., when the shooter is approaching on the Trapper side on a 2-on-1 or on a severe angle shot).

All goaltenders will find success with these two game situations if you position the Trapper in the *HIGH-FIVE POSITION* protecting the top corner on these short-side offensive attacks.

CHAPTER 13 - USING THE BLOCKER

Blocker saves are extremely productive during game situations. Two basic Blocker saves are discussed below.

1. Trapping The Puck: This occurs when goaltenders have enough time to *trap pucks* up against their Blockers with their Trappers. This decision, which makes for a great save, does not allow any rebounds to pop out in front as the puck is trapped safely.

2. Deflecting The Puck: This occurs when goaltenders are required to control a puck that has been shot *too hard* to trap it with the Trapper.

Goaltenders MUST *deflect the puck away* (e.g., over the glass or into the corner). In order to deflect the puck to the side, goaltenders must turn their wrists at the exact time when the puck makes contact with the Blockers. Goaltenders MUST watch the puck all the way!

The Blocker can be a valuable piece of equipment as long as goaltenders think about where they want to control the rebounds prior to making Blocker saves (e.g., where the opposing players are not located).

As with the Trapper, the Blocker should be in sight at all times. It should be out in front a bit, not uncomfortably close to the body. This allows for more freedom of movement and for goaltenders to watch the puck easily as it makes contact with the Blocker.

PART FOUR

PERFECTING
GAME SITUATIONS

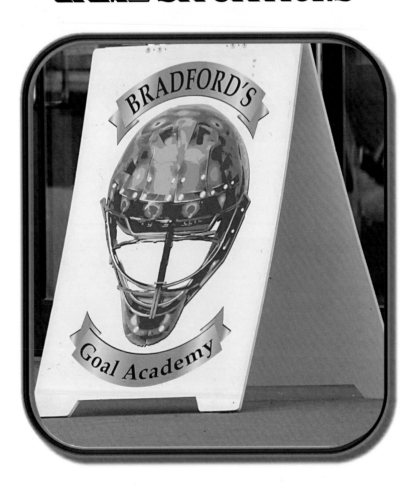

CHAPTER 14 - HUGGING THE POST

Goaltenders MUST learn to *hug the posts* properly. *Hugging the Post* is a defensive position which allows goaltenders to defend the net from severe angle shots when the puck is near the corner or behind the net. Goaltenders must be prepared to *explode out* to challenge the shooter that is receiving a pass from the corner or from behind the net.

IMPORTANT NOTE: After reading this chapter on Hugging the Post, we recommend that you also read the chapter on **SEVERE ANGLE SHOTS** (see Chapter 23) which will provide even more important detailed instruction concerning this special goaltender skill.

Educated goaltenders MUST be able to discourage opposing players from passing the puck from behind the net to the slot area. In order for this to happen, a goaltender MUST:

1. have proper positioning of his/her body and Goal Stick
2. have the majority of his/her body positioned inside the net with a balanced stance ready to *explode out* if a pass to the slot area occurs

This defensive positioning will prevent a puck from deflecting into the net if it hits the outside edge of the Goal Pad. The Goal Pads are slightly spread out in order for goaltenders to maintain good balance, with the outside Goal Pad held up against the inside of the post. This transfers the goaltender's weight to the post foot so that the leg is loaded and ready to **explode out**!

Trapper Side: The outside part of the heel of the skate should be held snuggly up against the inside of the post which will prevent any openings along the ice and the Trapper-side arm should be wrapped around the outside of the post. This will prevent goaltenders from being knocked away from the post. The heel of the goal stick should be held tightly to the toe of the Trapper-side skate.

Blocker Side: The outside part of the heel of the skate should be held snuggly up against the inside of the post which will prevent any openings along the ice and the Blocker-side arm should be wrapped around the outside of the post. This will prevent goaltenders from being knocked away from the post. The Trapper should be out ready to catch any high passes. The heel of the Goal Stick should be flat on the ice against the post.

Goaltenders that are positioned properly should be able to see the player in the corner or behind the net and read his/her next pass. In order to read the next pass, goaltenders must watch the player's eyes and body movement for any indications that show where he/she might be thinking about passing the puck.

ATTENTION GOALTENDERS: You must keep your skates hugging the inside of the post in order to prevent the puck from being poked in on the short side.

DO NOT GO FISHING! Goaltenders MUST not stretch out their bodies before the pass to the slot area is made.

 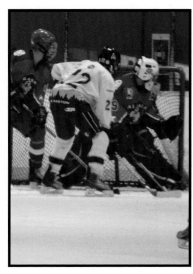

Elite goaltenders will be able to read the pass with an educated anticipation knowing where and when to intercept these passes.

- ✓ Any passes that travel through the crease should be stopped by goaltenders.
- ✓ Any passes headed toward the slot area that travel outside the crease and outside the goaltender's reach should be left alone; goaltenders must simply ***explode out to challenge the pass-out!***

IMPORTANT NOTE: Goaltenders MUST maintain proper body alignment when *hugging the post.* They should be prepared to *explode out* as well as prepared to *deflect a pass* that may occur (without stretching their bodies too far - *fishing for the puck!*).

They should be prepared to move laterally to the other post by sideways shuffling while maintaining eye contact on the puck. It is best to look through the net (or over the net ... if you are tall enough) at the puck rather that over the net at the player as this will allow goaltenders to maintain the proper **Ready (SET) Position.**

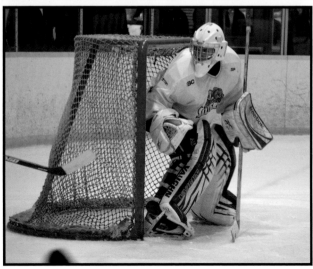

Goaltenders are faced with the game developing in front of them approximately 40% of the time. They are required to deal with the puck when it is **behind the net** or **in the corners of the ice surface** during the other 60% of the time.

We can safely say that it was **Wayne "The Great One" Gretzky** who established **his Office** effectively behind the goal net. Following the puck when it is behind the goal net has caused great difficulties for goaltenders that have had minimal experience with this game situation.

We have developed the most valuable method for **elite** goaltenders to reach high levels of success whenever the player takes the puck behind the goal net. We have carried out intensive research (e.g., studying videotaped recordings and actual playing experiences) in order to establish this method.

IMPORTANT TIP: As a goaltender prepares to move **from Post to Post** he/she MUST NOT turn his/her head while following the puck as it is being carried around the back of the net.

This simple *skill set* ensures that the goaltender keeps his/her eyes on the puck and the puck carrier during the critical moments where

Gretzky-like impersonators attempt to confuse him/her by reversing their path suddenly.

When the goaltender reaches the far post and is assured that the puck carrier is totally committed to travelling fully around the goal net, he/she can then be confident enough to turn his/her head around to search for the puck carrier coming out the other side.

This POST to POST movement must be practiced faithfully throughout the entire hockey season. The goaltender's head movements must become automatically correct 100% of the time! Coaches will be required to pay close attention to their goaltender's proper execution of this specific game situation during practice trials.

IMPORTANT NOTE: Constant reminders, specific constructive feedback, and even video-taped practices will greatly assist in providing a positive learning experience for goaltenders.

LISTEN UP: Hopefully the coaching staff will include game situation drills daily/weekly that will provide goaltenders with productive opportunities to move from POST to POST and to follow plays that occur behind the goal net!

Educated Goaltenders make ELITE GOALTENDERS!

Did You Know ...

Tim Thomas of the Boston Bruins began his NHL career at 28 years old. Since then he has collected some of the most notable hardware in the NHL (some on more than one occasion) including the: Stanley Cup, Conn Smythe, Vezina, Roger Crozier Saving Grace Award and has been an NHL All-Star. He has achieved all this after attending the University of Vermont on a Hockey Scholarship and playing a few seasons in Minor Pro and overseas. HE NEVER GAVE UP!

CHAPTER 16 - WRAP AROUNDS - *Paddle-Down Technique*

IMPORTANT NOTE: A tremendous amount of goals are scored during a hockey season when an offensive player wraps the puck quickly around the net.

Building upon the chapter that teaches goaltenders how to move from *Post to Post*, we will now turn to teaching the *Paddle-Down Technique* in order to prevent Wrap Around shots from scoring.

Using the *Paddle-Down Technique* allows the goaltender's gloves to be in close proximity to any loose pucks; the goaltender can quickly cover any dangerous rebounds.

As the goaltender uses the butterfly save technique during this game situation, the leg pad is positioned TIGHTLY against the inside of the post and the stick helps to hold the goaltender SOLIDLY against the post!

Often, the puck carrier will try to go around the goaltender on a Wrap Around and shoot the puck into the far side *instead* of trying to jam the puck into the net at the near post. Using the *Paddle-Down Technique* allows a goaltender to push the stick out toward the puck productively thereby following the puck across the front of the crease to make the save.

LISTEN UP: Coaches are encouraged to implement the Wrap Around game situation drill into team practices frequently.

This will definitely provide your goaltenders with opportunities to build confidence and reliability in making a Wrap Around save successfully; many potential goals throughout the hockey season will not occur due to extensive practice surrounding this essential *skill set*!

CHAPTER 17 - PASS-OUTS

Chapters 13, 14, and 15 describe unique skills that are required for *elite goaltenders* to guard against plays from behind the net.

ATTENTION *ELITE* GOALTENDERS: We have yet another very important game situation that needs to be mastered when the puck begins from behind the net or from the corners of the ice surface!

Opposing teams establish aggressive fore-checking systems regularly. These team systems lead to PASS-OUTS into the *slot area* and/or to the *points!* Goaltenders play a vital role in preventing plays such as these from turning into goals against!

There are four key points to consider when defending against a PASS-OUT:

1. Preparation
2. Anticipation
3. Execution
4. Finalization

PREPARATION - Goaltenders will find brief moments, while the puck is being fought over in the corners and/or behind the net, when they will process **ALL** the potential plays that are about to develop in front of them. ***This is the time to be fully prepared to EXPLODE off the post!***

ATTENTION GOALTENDERS: Establish a STRONG, FULLY LOADED (coiled snake-like) leg which is perfectly hugging the post. Proper weight transfer will assure that you get a *coiled leg*. Focus on putting most of your body weight on the post foot.

As you wait on the post, you are already standing on the inside edge of your goal skate and directing your body weight onto the front tip of the skate blade.

IMPORTANT NOTE: There are two different game situations that need to be discussed in great detail. There is a massive difference between a situation when a player decides to pass the puck out to the **high slot** (i.e., out high) as opposed to the **top of the crease** (i.e., in tight).

ELITE goaltenders are able to differentiate between these two high-percentage scoring plays and set themselves up according to where the puck travels.

Game Situation #1 - *Pass-Out To The High Slot*. When a puck is passed out from the corner or behind the goal line to an offensive player in the high slot, the goaltender MUST begin by Hugging the Post (see Chapter 13). He/she MUST **EXPLODE** off the post using his/her most confident stance while remaining up on his/her feet. The goaltender's stance may be either a Butterfly Stance or a Solid Stand-Up Stance whichever provides him/her with the most success on shots from the high slot.

EXPLODING OUT to the top of the crease, while centering on the puck, helps the goaltender to arrive in time to make the proper save on shots taken from the high slot. Once the goaltender arrives at the top of the crease, he/she will be fully prepared in the **Ready (SET) Position** to stop the high-percentage scoring opportunity.

If the shot from the high slot approaches the net LOW to the ice, the goaltenders must become fully prepared to cover the entire ice level. While covering the **LOW** portion of the net completely, *elite* goaltenders are now prepared to focus solely on any potential **HIGH** shots from the high slot.

PROTECT LOW, LOOK HIGH!

IMPORTANT NOTE: If the goaltender decides to go down as the puck is traveling toward the high slot, the shooter will have plenty of holes to shoot at in this quick bang-bang play, *even if the puck is high in the slot area.*

The goaltender MUST arrive at the top of the crease prior to deciding to go down onto his/her knees.

Game Situation #2 - *Pass-Out To The Top Of The Crease.* When a puck is passed out from the corner or behind the goal line to an offensive player at the top of the crease, the goaltender MUST **cover the bottom portion of the net extremely quickly** while still maintaining coverage of the upper portion of the net.

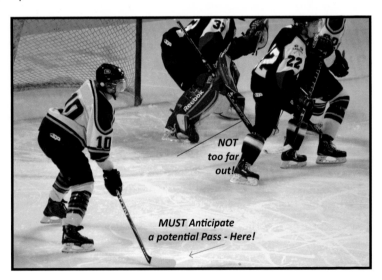

NOT too far out!

MUST Anticipate a potential Pass - Here!

IMPORTANT NOTE: While starting the initial play by Hugging the Post properly (see Chapter 13), the goaltender MUST learn to anticipate where the Pass-Out will travel to (i.e., the **high slot** or the **top of the crease**). Once the goaltender begins to anticipate a Pass-Out to the top of the crease, he/she MUST place the outside knee onto the ice allowing that same outside leg to move quickly across the net. This goaltending strategy immediately produces the necessary far-post coverage on these **bang-bang** and **tip-in plays**. These dangerous plays occur when the puck is passed in tight, at the top of the crease.

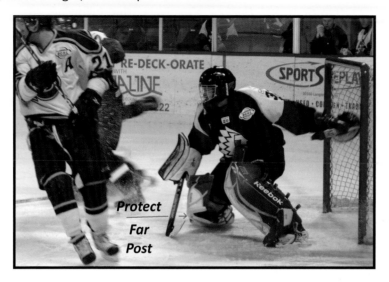

Setting up like this (i.e., PREPARATION) lessens the reaction time effectively, which is required to EXPLODE out aggressively! Being **PREPARED to EXPLODE** out dramatically reduces the valuable time that is necessary in order to follow the **Pass-Out**.

ANTICIPATION - Technical knowledge and experience combine to create this most sought after skill in the field of **Elite Goaltending**! Listen to every older, retired, ex-elite goaltender discuss their careers and you will soon recognize that they ALL state, *"If I only knew then, what I know NOW!"*

Anticipating the play correctly provides educated goaltenders with an amazing advantage!

This skill includes:

1. knowing **WHEN** the puck is about to be passed out
2. knowing **WHERE** the puck will be passed out to
3. knowing **HOW** the puck will be directed back at the goaltender
4. knowing **WHICH** save method will be required based upon the type of shot that is about to occur

A COMMON QUESTION AROUND THE HOCKEY WORLD

How do you LEARN or TEACH to ANTICIPATE effectively?

To learn the **Game of Hockey** effectively, the following are some essential strategies:

1. study game films
2. read research articles or expertly written books on goaltending
3. attend live games where **your** focus and thoughts are totally ***zoned in*** on the goaltender alone as the play surrounds him/her

IMPORTANT NOTE: There is no simple way to learn to *anticipate* correctly! The answer is: ***Study, study, study!!!*** *Learn the play! Learn the game!*

EXECUTION - Now that you are all *SET* to EXPLODE off the post, the time has come to discuss *WHERE* to go. There are three possible choices at this point:

1. **EXPLODE** down to the ice immediately with a ***Paddle-Down Save*** if you are anticipating an immediate shot from close range on your short side
2. **EXPLODE** down to the ice immediately with a ***Pad Save*** if you are anticipating an immediate shot aimed along the ice to the far post
3. **EXPLODE** out *challenging* and *centering* on the shot in your butterfly stance as you anticipate the direction of the pass into the *slot* or back to the *points*

ATTENTION GOALTENDERS: Using your very valuable developed skill of intelligent anticipation will do you little good unless you are totally prepared to EXPLODE off the post during a Pass-Out play! Simply moving away from the post is insufficient and will result in a number of pucks going into the net! ***DON'T LET THIS HAPPEN TO YOU!***

FINALIZATION - Once goaltenders have produced a successful save on a dangerous *Pass-Out* play, the next responsibility is to FINALIZE the play by controlling all Rebounds! Learning to become the *stingiest* goaltender in the league is a reputation one longs to receive. Goaltenders that fight hard and win the battles for all loose pucks consistently will make a significant difference in their team's ***Win/Loss Category***!

REPUTATION IS KEY! Combining high levels of confidence with a tremendous skill in catching virtually every shot will give goaltenders another great reputation! Opposing players will soon realize that there are rarely any rebounds when the Trapper is used to catch the puck!

SUMMARY: Learning to play Pass-Outs properly, as described above, provides *elite goaltenders* with opportunities to *SHINE* in the nets!

Cash in on these opportunities;
ensure that you advance to the next levels in hockey!

CHAPTER 18 - WALK-OUTS FROM THE CORNERS

When players **walk out from the corner** with the puck, goaltenders must quickly prepare to identify the best course of action. Goaltenders that want to be recognized as **elite** goaltenders MUST fully understand the differences that are created when players **walk out from either corner** (e.g., the left wing corner or the right wing corner). Whether a player is left-handed or right-handed has a significant effect on how the **walk-out** should be handled by goaltenders.

The four game situations listed below, which are extremely common, describe how different players should be assessed and handled by goaltenders during **walk-outs.**

IMPORTANT NOTE: The scenarios which are described below are for goaltenders that **catch** with their **left hand only!** (Goaltenders that catch with their right hand will be addressed later in this chapter).

GAME SITUATION #1 *From The Left-Wing Corner:* When a **left-handed** player walks out to the net from the left-wing corner, the puck will be carried **between** the player's body and the goaltender as the player walks out and cuts across the top of the crease area.

Using an **EXPLOSIVE** Poke Check would be the key choice in stopping this walk-out effectively (see Chapter 10) especially if the player walks out **tight to the net.**

GAME SITUATION #2 *From The <u>Same</u> Left-Wing Corner:* When a ***right-handed*** player walks out to the net from the ***left-wing corner*** (called their ***off-wing***), the players' body will be shielding the puck as the player walks out in front of the net. A Poke Check should **NOT** be attempted on this type of play; it is not as simple to Poke Check through the player's skates.

We recommend that ***elite*** goaltenders play this game situation by, first of all, ***hugging the post*** properly and then deciding, if the puck is brought in tight to the net, to go into the *one knee down position* to gain a sufficient amount of low net coverage. A Butterfly Crawl will help the goaltender move across the crease properly with the player. The player walking out towards the net may choose one of three options when on his/her forehand:

1. shoot the puck to any spot on the short side that appears open
2. fake the shot and try to carry the puck around the goaltender to the far post
3. fake the shot and try to carry the puck around the goaltender to the short side

IMPORTANT NOTE: When moving laterally across the crease in the Butterfly Crawl, goaltenders must pay close attention to being tight through the body so **no holes** open up for the puck to squeeze through. Goaltenders must always follow the path of the puck with the blade of their Goal Stick.

SPECIAL NOTE: If a *right-handed* player (above) walks out to the net from the *Off-Wing* (the left-wing corner), on his/her backhand, goaltenders can treat them as if they were a left-handed player; hence, an **EXPLOSIVE** Poke Check would be the save to *nail them* with!

IMPORTANT NOTE: The scenarios described below are for goaltenders that *catch* with their *left hand only!* (Goaltenders that catch with their right hand will be addressed later in this chapter).

*Right-handed Player ...
cutting in from
RIGHT Wing!*

GAME SITUATION #3 *From The Right-Wing Corner*: When a *right-handed* player walks out to the net from the right-wing corner, the puck will be carried *between* the player's body and the goaltender as the player cuts across the top of the crease area. The player walking out towards the net may choose one of the three options when on his/her forehand:

1. shoot the puck to the top corner, short side, or over the goaltender's shoulder
2. tap the puck between the goaltender's legs through the 5-hole
3. fake the shot and skate around the goaltender to the far post

If the right-handed player attempts to walk out of the right-wing corner by skating close to the goaltender, an **EXPLOSIVE** *Sweep Check* would be the key choice in save techniques to stop this walk-out effectively.

Right-Handed Player walking out of the RIGHT corner!

Considering the "Sweep Check"

GAME SITUATION #4 *From The <u>Same</u> Right-Wing Corner*: When a **left-handed** player walks out to the net from the right-wing corner, the goaltender should follow the same goaltending procedures listed above (see: **GAME SITUATION #2 from the <u>Same</u> Left-Wing Corner**: earlier in this chapter).

GOALTENDERS THAT CATCH WITH THE RIGHT HAND

IMPORTANT NOTE: The scenarios that were described above must be read with an opposite mindset for goaltenders that *catch* with the ***right hand***!

1. *Right-handed* players walking out to the net from the right-wing corner may be Poke Checked, etc.

2. *Left-handed* players walking out to the net from the left-wing corner may be Sweep Checked or followed across the crease.

When these game situations arise, goaltenders MUST be prepared to:

1. stop a shot from a severe angle
2. move across the crease laterally (e.g., Butterfly Crawl) in order to follow the player if he/she decides to skate across the top of the crease striving to get around the goaltender
   NOTE: *The Butterfly Crawl, when executed properly, provides goaltenders with a sufficient amount of low net coverage while maintaining protection of the upper portion of the net as the puck is located in tight and cannot see a direct line over the goaltender into the net.*
3. get to the far post quickly if the player decides to turn the **walk-out** into a **wrap-around** situation by going around the net

IMPORTANT NOTE: When moving laterally across the crease in the Butterfly Crawl, goaltenders must pay close attention to being tight through the body so **no holes** open up for the puck to squeeze through.

ATTENTION GOALTENDERS: *Walk-outs* will occur many times during your career! You may potentially be run over by a player that walks out hard to the net and loses his balance *(intentionally)*.

It is important that you expect this to happen and that you do not get upset when players run into you! Your teammates will *take care of business* if the opposing team tries to **throw you off your game!**

A Coach Brent Bradford and Coach Vic LeMire Reminder:

Be strong!

Stand your ground!

Become very effective and knowledgeable when it comes to game situations when players walk out from the corners!

CHAPTER 19 - PLAYERS DRIVING IN FROM THE WING

Those that want to be recognized as *elite* goaltenders MUST fully understand the differences that are created when players *drive hard to the net* from the left-wing or right-wing of the ice surface. Whether a player is left-handed or right-handed has a significant effect on how the **net-drive** should be handled by goaltenders.

The four game situations listed below, which are extremely common, describe how different players should be assessed and handled by goaltenders during *net-drives*.

IMPORTANT NOTE: The scenarios described below are for goaltenders that *catch* with their *left hand only!* (A goaltender that catches with his/her right hand will be addressed later in this chapter).

GAME SITUATION #1 *From The Left-Wing:* When a *left-handed* player is driving hard to the net from the left-wing, the puck will be carried *between* the player's body and the goaltender as the player cuts across the high crease area.

Using an **EXPLOSIVE** Poke Check would be the key choice in stopping this net-drive effectively (see Chapter 10), especially if the player cuts in tight to the net.

GAME SITUATION #2 *From The __Same__ Left-Wing:* When a ***right-handed*** player is driving hard to the net from the ***left- wing,*** (called their ***off-wing***), the player's body will be shielding the puck as the player drives hard across the top of the goal crease. A Poke Check should ***NOT*** be attempted on this type of play because it is not as simple to Poke Check through the player's skates.

We recommend that ***elite*** goaltenders play this game situation similarly to a breakaway by first challenging out, then, begin skating backwards trying to match the player's speed (see Chapter 25). A Butterfly Crawl save will help the goaltender move across the crease properly with the player. The player driving towards the net may choose one of these three options when on his/her forehand:

1. shoot the puck to any spot that appears open
2. fake the shot and try to carry the puck around the goaltender to the far post
3. fake the shot and try to carry the puck around the goaltender to the short-side

IMPORTANT NOTE: When moving laterally across the crease in the Butterfly Crawl, goaltenders must pay close attention to being tight through the body so ***no holes*** open up for the puck to squeeze through. Goaltenders must always follow the path of the puck with the blade of their Goal Stick.

SPECIAL NOTE: If a *right-handed* player is cutting in on the *Off-Wing* (the left-wing) and is deep on his/her backhand, goaltenders can treat him/her just as if he/she were a left-handed player; hence, an **EXPLOSIVE** Poke Check would be the save to *nail them* with!

IMPORTANT NOTE: The scenarios described below are for goaltenders that *catch* with their *left hand only!* (A goaltender that catches with his/her right hand will be addressed later in this chapter).

Sweep Check ... or, follow Player across

GAME SITUATION #3 *From The Right-Wing:* When a **right-handed** player is driving hard to the net from the right-wing, the puck will be carried **between** the player's body and the goaltender as the player cuts across the high crease area. Using an **EXPLOSIVE** Sweep Check would be the key choice in stopping this net-drive effectively, especially if the player cuts in tight to the net.

GAME SITUATION #4 *From The <u>Same</u> Right-Wing*: When a *left-handed* player is driving to the net from the right-wing, the goaltender would follow the same goaltending procedures listed above (see: **GAME SITUATION #2** *from the <u>Same</u> Left-Wing* earlier in this chapter).

IMPORTANT NOTE: The scenarios described above must be read with an opposite mindset for goaltenders that *catch* with the **right hand**!

1. *Right-handed* players driving to the net from the right-wing may be Poke Checked, etc.
2. *Left-handed* players driving to the net from the left- wing may be Sweep Checked or played like a Breakaway, etc.

When these game situations arise, the goaltender must be prepared to:

1. stop a shot from an angle (potentially a severe angle)
2. move across the crease laterally (e.g., Butterfly Crawl) in order to follow the shooter if he/she decides to skate across the top of the crease striving to get around the goaltender
   NOTE: *The Butterfly Crawl, when executed properly, will provide the goaltender with a sufficient amount of low net coverage while maintaining protection of the upper portion of the net.*

3. get to the far post quickly if the player decides to turn the **net-drive** into a **wrap-around** situation by going around the net

ATTENTION GOALTENDERS: *Net-Drives* will occur many times during your career! You may potentially be run over by a player that drives hard to the net and loses his balance.

It is important that you expect this to happen and that you do not get upset when players run over you! Your teammates will *take care of business* if the other team tries that!

A Coach Brent Bradford and Coach Vic LeMire Reminder:

Be strong!

Stand your ground!

Become very effective and knowledgeable when it comes to game situations when players drive hard to net from the wing!

In continuing our mission to help create *intelligent goaltenders*, (e.g., those that continually STUDY and understand the Game of Hockey), we will now turn to an extremely common game situation where the play causes the puck carrier to change direction and begin skating horizontally (i.e., **east to west**) across the top of the slot area with the puck.

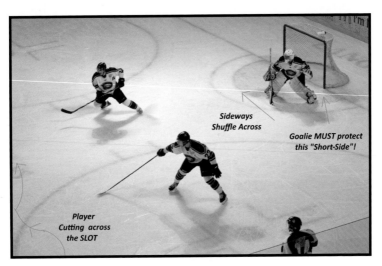

Sideways Shuffle Across

Goalie MUST protect this "Short-Side"!

Player Cutting across the SLOT

Game Situation Explained: A basic 1-on-1 play coming down the wing along the sideboards towards the goaltender. The puck carrier suddenly hits the breaks and pivots towards the middle of the ice with the puck.

Goaltender Positioning: Goaltenders should challenge out to the TOP of the goal crease. As the player carries the puck high across the slot area in front of the goaltender, the goaltender MUST follow him/her while being prepared in the **Ready (SET) Position** at every moment for a sudden shot. This situation causes certain difficulties that we are now going to examine and solve for goaltenders.

The Puck-Carrier's Plan #1: Make the goaltender move across the front of the net too soon and shoot to the vacated short-side!

Our Proven Solution: For success during this game situation, the goaltender must demonstrate **serious patience** by WAITING a split second before beginning to shuffle across to follow the shooter! By hesitating slightly like this, the goaltender protects the short-side entirely (i.e., where players like to shoot at) and makes the save while moving in the opposite direction. This is normally a very difficult save to make; shooters know this! Delaying the Sideways Shuffle greatly improves the goaltender's success on this play. As the goaltender delays like this, he/she must now focus on any shots to the long-side knowing that the short-side is well protected.

The Puck-Carrier's Plan #2: Catch the goaltender with wide-open legs as I move across the slot area and shoot the puck through the 5-hole!

Our Proven Solution: Properly trained goaltenders will learn to use the Sideways Shuffle to move across while watching carefully **ALL** of the shooter's arm and leg movements. *Intelligent goaltenders* watch for weight transfer in the shooter's body indicating that a shot is imminent! While ***CHALLENGING OUT*** properly, an educated goaltender executes an ***EXPLOSIVE*** butterfly save while controlling all rebounds!

PART FIVE

MASTERING
SPECIALTY SKILLS

CHAPTER 21 - REBOUNDS

REBOUND is a word that goaltenders detest just as much as the word **GOAL!** Goaltenders must develop the skills, knowledge, and attitude to **control almost every shot that they face**. Elite-level hockey demands goaltenders to reduce the number of loose pucks that are left out in front of the net. Goaltenders need to approach each and every game with the relentless desire to restrict the opposing team to a single shot whenever a scoring chance occurs.

BAD REBOUNDS: In order for goaltenders to improve their game and turn losses into wins by bringing down their **Goals Against Average** (i.e., GAA), they must strive to **diminish all bad rebounds** by controlling pucks from the initial shot. Goaltenders must approach each and every shot with the attitude that it will be **"the end of the play!"**

Prime examples of **Bad Rebounds** are when:

➢ pucks go off the Trapper and lie out in front of the crease
➢ pucks that hit goaltenders in the mid-section and drop to the ice
➢ pucks that are shot from a distance and are kicked back out front

IMPORTANT NOTE: Goaltenders must recognize that there will always be situations during a game when they do everything they can just to get a piece of their equipment in front of the puck. These saves are not classified as bad rebounds. However, **elite** goaltenders are able to control rebounds in these situations due to their relentless hard work toward developing the skills, knowledge, attitude, and conditioning in order to stay in control even when the play forces them to be out of control! *Elite* goaltenders are able to control rebounds without even thinking about it!

ATTENTION GOALTENDERS: Becoming a *very stingy thief* and *aggressive* on all loose pucks will generate more wins for your team!

GOOD REBOUNDS: *The best rebound is NO REBOUND!* However, when a goaltender cannot help but allow a rebound to occur, he/she must send the puck into a *safe zone!*

Point Shots In The Air: If the puck is traveling toward the goaltender in the air, he/she can either catch the puck or deflect it high into the stands. Both of these goaltender decisions will generate a stoppage in play (see Chapter 10, 11, and 12).

Point Shots Along The Ice: If the puck is traveling toward the goaltender hard along the ice, he/she can deflect the puck into one of the *safe zones* in the corners in order to provide his/her team with time to regroup or deflect it up into the netting for a stoppage in play (see Chapter 10).

Shots From The Wing: It is important for goaltenders to fully understand that shots from the wing will almost always result in a rebound due to the close proximity of the shooter. In this situation, goaltenders must maintain effective positioning and accurate angles while being prepared in the proper **Ready (SET) Position** in order to react to the shot and to keep any potential rebounds in front of them (not toward the slot area).

Loose Pucks In Front: Goaltenders must become knowledgeable about deciding when to *pounce on loose pucks* that are laying in front of them. Goaltenders must quickly pull the puck back in towards them with their goal sticks so that the opposing players cannot beat them to loose pucks. It is important for **goaltenders *to not punch loose pucks*** back out into the slot area.

ATTENTION GOALTENDERS: There are situations during a game when sending a rebound out in front of the crease area is the safest decision!

When Your Team Is Short-Handed: The safest place to kick a rebound from a point shot is to the area in front of the net during a short-handed situation. This might sound strange, but if you look at this situation closely you will recognize the fact that you have four teammates to their one or two in that area of the ice.

This advantage of manpower should provide your team with a good opportunity to clear the puck out of the zone. The opposition is spread out around the perimeter during their power-play which will make it vitally important that rebounds are not sent into the corners or to the side boards. This will allow the opposing team to regain puck control again!

BECOME A REBOUND MASTER! *Elite* goaltenders have become **masters** when it comes to controlling rebounds. They are capable of making proper decisions when the puck is heading towards them prior to making the initial save! **ALL** goaltenders must practice controlling rebounds during every team practice, so that when it comes time for a game, rebound control is not a problem!

POINT-TO-POINT ONE-TIMERS: Goaltenders MUST learn to anticipate this common game situation with great precision and mobility. A short-handed penalty kill is the prime game situation when ***point-to-point one-timers*** occur. Goaltenders cannot get caught too far out of the net as they set up for the original point shot.

POINT-TO-HALF BOARDS ONE-TIMERS: Goaltenders MUST learn to anticipate this similar common game situation with great precision and mobility. A short-handed penalty kill is another prime game situation when *point-to-half boards one-timers* occur. Goaltenders cannot get caught too far out of the net as they set up for the original point shot.

IMPORTANT NOTE: A Butterfly Slide is most effective with these two types of one-timed shots! The only chance goaltenders have to stop a very dangerous scoring opportunity like these require the following *elite* techniques:

1. proper initial positioning
2. educated anticipation of the pass
3. **EXPLOSIVE** driving of the leg pad down low and across to the far post

ATTENTION GOALTENDERS: You should catch all point shots that are traveling in the air. This provides your team with an opportunity to take a whistle and to get a new line out for the face-off as the original line may have been tired and running around.

BE AWARE: A dangerous situation that *WILL* undoubtedly occur is whenever a slap shot is taken from the point and it drifts *wide* of the net! In this situation, goaltenders that are out challenging must get back to the post quickly and must read the bounce off the back boards. The boards behind the nets can be very lively allowing pucks to bounce back in front of the net quickly!

If goaltenders are not attentive to the potential rebound off the back boards, they will observe players scoring in the open nets because they are still outside the crease where they were originally challenging from!

DO NOT GET CAUGHT SLEEPING ON THIS PLAY!

GET BACK TO THE POST QUICKLY WHEN A POINT SHOT DRIFTS WIDE OF THE NET!

A Bradford/LeMire Homework Assignment

Try to name as many former NHL goaltenders that have become hockey analysts (e.g., television, radio, internet, etc.). Write down, next to your list of names, why you believe they are so effective in that line of work. Hint: Kelly Hrudey is an amazing hockey analyst, but he is not the only former NHL goaltender in that line of work! Note: We did not limit this assignment solely to NHL analysts.

CHAPTER 22 - SCREENED SHOTS

Screened shots can involve a small or large amount of players standing in front of goaltenders as shots are taken from the points. Goaltenders must get used to being screened during game action. When defensemen shoot pucks toward the net through a crowd of players, they tend to shoot low on the ice because that is where the percentages lie for a potential goal. For the most part, the players' big upper bodies cover a large portion of the goaltender's upper part of the net. For this reason, it is to the goaltender's benefit that a solid butterfly save or a pad save is used to protect the lower parts of the net!

It is during these screened shot opportunities when goaltenders must **search for** and **find** the puck as it makes its way toward the net. **Elite** goaltenders find a way to get into a position where the puck will most likely squirt through and potentially enter the net. **Elite** goaltenders are able to look through a **lane** that exists between the shooters in front and the goaltenders. Finding the **lane** is crucial if goaltenders want to gain a sense as to where the shot will potentially be aimed toward.

IMPORTANT NOTE: Goaltenders must remain standing in a low **Ready (SET) Position** as they search for the puck **and** the shooting actions of the shooter. **Goaltenders *must know WHEN* the screened shot** is on its way towards the net. Once the puck or the shot attempt has been located, goaltenders then choose their save selection as the puck begins its journey toward the net (e.g., butterfly save, pad save, stand up, etc.).

Do Not get "tied up" with the Traffic in front!

ATTENTION GOALTENDERS: It is very important that you do not get tied up in the traffic of players in front of you. You MUST maintain a high level of mobility in order to follow the puck laterally if it gets blocked or bounces loose. If you get tied up with the players, you will not be able to react properly to a puck that has squirted out to the left or to the right of you leaving an open net for an opposing player to shoot at.

FAKE SHOTS TO A PASS: When *elite* goaltenders begin to earn the reputation of being stellar goaltenders, opposing players and coaches will discuss the fact that goals are rarely scored from shots that are taken by the initial puck carrier. Team strategies will be discussed and developed such as, *We need to get around the goaltender, fake a shot, and then pass it across to a teammate!*

YOU HAVE MADE A GREAT NAME FOR YOURSELF! When coaches from opposing teams agree that in order to score goals against you, their players need to get the puck around you, you MUST fully understand that they *highly respect you* as a goaltender!

When a *fake shot to a pass* occurs during game action, *elite* goaltenders separate themselves from goaltenders that have not reached *elite* status. This is quite noticeable. *Elite* goaltenders *anticipate* the *fake shot to a pass* decision and travel laterally across the crease area with either an explosive T-Push or an electrifying Butterfly Slide. Both

150

of these movements provide goaltenders with the ability to get across and prepared in time for a potential one-timer from the puck receiver.

IMPORTANT NOTE: Goaltenders that work hard on a consistent basis to **MASTER** goaltender-specific skating skills will be rewarded when an opposing player fakes a shot and passes it across to a teammate. Goaltenders that do not believe goaltender-specific skating skills are important will be observed *diving across the net* in a desperate attempt to save one-timers which usually go into empty nets. However, when the shooter hits the diving goaltender by *luck* and the crowd goes wild because they believe this was a tremendous save, the goaltender has absolutely no rebound control and the second shot usually scores!

ATTENTION GOALTENDERS: It is imperative that you reduce the amount of distance you challenge out in order to be effective in getting across the crease in time to stop one-timers that originate from a *fake shot to a pass*. Review the ODD/EVEN RULE (see Chapter 24).

What is **EXTRA EFFORT**? Goaltenders that **NEVER GIVE UP** on a seemingly non-stoppable shot will be rewarded with a save that truthfully should not have been made under normal circumstances! A special extra effort will quite often force the shooter to *rush a shot and MISS the net completely*.

CHAPTER 23 - THE *BAD ANGLE LINE*

Commonly referred to as **Playing the Angles,** goaltenders at **ALL** levels are required to perfect their angles and positioning as they confront an opposing shooter that is committed to taking a SHOT from one side of the ice surface or the other.

Over the years, there have been dozens of theories, strategies, and techniques developed for goaltenders in order to **SET-UP** properly on a Bad Angle shot. With over 60-plus years of combined goaltender teaching experience, coaches and authors Brent Bradford and Vic LeMire have developed this most valuable, yet simple, methodology for playing Bad Angle shots successfully!

It is called the *"BAD ANGLE" LINE!*

As pictured below, goaltenders should now refer to their angles and positioning according to this **Bad Angle Line.**

WHERE IS IT? The **Bad Angle Line** is *mentally painted* on the ice surface beginning on the goal line directly between the two goal posts. This straight line goes exactly through the face-off dot and continues out to the sideboards. **Intelligent goaltenders** will identify, on the sideboards, a particular *mark* or *advertisement* as an ending reference point for the **Bad Angle Line.**

The **Bad Angle Line** is the SAME on both sides of the ice surface (it is the SAME at both ends of the rink, as well). The only difference may be which side board reference mark a goaltender chooses as the ending point for the **Bad Angle Line** to be drawn when he/she changes ends to begin a new period of stopping pucks.

It is the responsibility of **ALL** goaltenders to review this line every time they step into the crease area on face-offs and during quiet time-out moments of the game.

HOW TO USE THE *BAD ANGLE LINE:* If the puck is located for a shot from directly ON TOP of the **Bad Angle Line**, the goaltender positions him/herself *directly over the line* in the most comfortable Butterfly Stance - challenging well outside the crease!

IMPORTANT NOTE: Goaltenders are most effective on these shots if they are prepared to **Protect Low** and **Look High**! That means they need to be prepared to produce a very solid butterfly save covering the entire width of the net along the ice with their leg pads and stick (***Protect Low***).

When they are in this effective *READY (SET) POSITION*, they are now ready to search for pucks that are shot high using their shoulders and gloves to cover the top corners of the net (***Look High***).

153

SPECIAL NOTE: Unknowingly, the shooters also use the Face-Off Dot as one of their favorite shooting reference points. This lends perfectly to the goaltenders' advantage for ideal positioning on **Bad Angle** shots.

1. If the puck is located for a shot from either side of the *Bad Angle Line*, the goaltender simply needs to adjust his/her positioning slightly sideways from the *Bad Angle Line*.
2. If the puck is located directly out in front of the net in the high slot area, an *educated goaltender* will position him/herself using the two following methods:
   a) the goaltender sets him/herself up directly between both *Bad Angle Lines*
   b) the goaltender will also use the straight line that extends directly between both hash marks originating in the middle of the net

Proper **ANGLES** and **POSITIONING Skills** during game action become extremely evident for **elite** goaltenders that have learned to mentally *paint* the three lines on the ice surface. They are able to apply these effective lines to stop *Bad Angle* shots consistently!

CONCLUSION: *Proper Challenging* and a *Strong Butterfly Stance* add to the advantage and success a goaltender has on the many **Bad Angle Shots** that occur during game action.

CHAPTER 24 - SEVERE ANGLE SHOTS

Somewhere, somehow a NEW theory suddenly developed in modern goaltending techniques. It is a theory which several goaltenders and their coaches have been instructed, and we dare say **mis-instructed,** on the best method to use in order to stop shots directed at the net from a severe angle originating from the corners of the ice surface and near the goal line.

To fully back up *our **severe criticism*** of this new method, we have exhaustedly researched the many attempts of goaltenders in every league, from Minor Hockey to the Professional ranks, as they unsuccessfully drop down to one knee on **Severe Angle** shots. One simply needs to recall the 2009/10 Stanley Cup overtime winning goal to understand how ineffective this NEW method of stopping **Severe Angle** shots has been proven to be!

It is unclear who developed this misguided, one-knee down positioning, but, *who* is not our concern! It is the goaltenders that struggle to stop **SEVERE ANGLE** shots, the ones that fail to remain SOLID up against the goal posts that WE really care about.

We shall illustrate through these *tell all* action pictures exactly why we must warn every goaltender about playing these shots correctly or incorrectly!

Please pay close attention to OUR *Severe Angle One-Knee Down* lesson:

Simply creating a **SOLID Legs-Closed Stand-Up Stance**, while correctly hugging the post with a slight turn towards the shot, will *guarantee* a goaltender *stops EVERY shot* from this area. This, our suggested method, will also keep the pucks continually in front of the goaltender.

Using our **PROVEN** method of stopping *Severe Angle* shots *will also protect against* giving up *soft goals* to the upper corner of the net on the short side!

THERE IS A TIME AND PLACE! Goaltender Coaches Brent Bradford and Vic LeMire do agree that using the **One-Knee Down Method** to make a save is effective ... *during the one specific game situation that is described below!*

Game Example: It is a play when a shooter decides to carry the puck out from behind or beside the net within a short distance of the goaltender. It is NOT a Wrap-Around play when the Paddle-Down Method is preferred, but, a play when the shooter has pulled away from the net slightly.

Utilizing the **One-Knee Down Method** would definitely permit goaltenders to cover the post area with one leg up and also cover the entire ice level with the far knee down. This may prevent a shot to the far post from going in (if the far leg pad is not tucked in which can be observed on a daily basis during Minor Hockey games).

NOTE: It is important for goaltenders to hold firm to the goal post, if possible, preventing soft short-side goals from going in. Although this same save can be made by stepping out to challenge the shooter, protecting the entire ice level is quite valuable.

In the picture above, it is evident that there is a hole between the Goal Pads for the puck to go through. This is a very soft goal that could have been easily avoided. Do you understand that, when this position is used ineffectively, pucks will be scored easily?

We find it absolutely infuriating to observe goaltenders dropping down into this position automatically the moment a player is heading toward him/her from the side boards. We too often find ourselves asking:

1. Does the goaltender know that there is a HUGE hole between his/her legs setting the shooter up for a *soft goal*?
2. Does the goaltender have absolutely any idea that his/her post skate is pulled well off the post setting the shooter up for a *soft goal*?
3. Does the goaltender understand that the whole top of the net ... and the far side ... is WIDE open setting the shooter up for a *soft goal* from a distant shot?

STORY TIME! The following is a short story that describes a specific situation concerning a goaltender during an **elite** hockey team tryout camp.

THE TRYOUT CAMP: During a final scrimmage when all the hockey evaluators were sitting in the stands making notes, a young Peewee goaltender stood in the crease giving 100% effort. He was performing very well and was selected as one of the top four goaltenders. In fact, the four goaltenders were rated so closely, a simple mistake could have made the difference to either making the team or not.

A SIMPLE MISTAKE HAPPENED! Near the end of the scrimmage, an offensive player skated down the side boards and cut in toward the net and prepared himself to shoot from a severe angle. As he prepared to release the shot, I noticed the goaltender that was initially challenging the shooter went back quickly to his post and dropped his outside (i.e., long-side) knee. There were no players in front of the net for the shooter to pass to, so a shot was imminent.

Simply, STAND UP ... get SOLID!

I AM IN MY POSITION - I DO NOT NEED TO REACT! The goaltender went into the *One-Knee Down Position* giving the shooter a huge amount of net to shoot at. *I thought, "Why is the goaltender in the **One-Knee Down Position** and not challenging the shooter?"* As the shot was taken, the goaltender, with his glove placed over his pad as if he believed his decision was perfectly executed, watched the puck get released and continued to watch it go straight over his glove into the short-side top corner! He remained in the **One-Knee Down Position** and did not react at all to the puck which *he watched go straight into the net!*

GOAL! As I looked around at the evaluators, I observed them marking the goal down. They probably did not even notice that with a little bit of proper education, that goaltender could have easily stopped that shot ... but he did not and that ended up being a deciding factor in the final roster. That goaltender let one more goal in than all the others!

QUESTION PERIOD

1. What should the goaltender have done in this situation?
2. Do you believe the goaltender was properly assessed in this situation by the evaluators?
3. Does it matter that this young goaltender has not yet been taught the most effective method of stopping simple shots from a severe angle?

ATTENTION GOALTENDERS!

React to the puck!

CHAPTER 25 - ODD/EVEN RULE

Where Is The Shot Coming From? The ODD/EVEN Rule is extremely important for goaltenders to learn to understand. Many times during game action, goaltenders are *called upon* to read plays, stop pucks, and control rebounds from opposing attacks that originate outside the blue line or near center ice (e.g., ODD-MAN or EVEN-MAN OFFENSIVE ATTACKS).

1. ODD-MAN OFFENSIVE ATTACK: This particular game situation occurs when there are more opposing players on the offensive attack than the number of defensive players who are defending the attack. Common game situations, such as; 2-on-1, 3-on-2 are classified as **ODD-MAN OFFENSIVE ATTACKS**.

ODD-MAN RULE: Goaltenders MUST be prepared in the Ready (SET) Position and remain at the top of the crease while reading the play when an **ODD-MAN OFFENSIVE ATTACK** begins to develop during a game.

IMPORTANT NOTE: Goaltenders MUST never get caught standing outside the crease during an **ODD-MAN OFFENSIVE ATTACK**. If this happens, they will be in danger of having the puck passed around them to the open offensive player.

2. EVEN-MAN OFFENSIVE ATTACK: This particular game situation occurs when there is the same amount of opposing players on the offensive attack as there are defensive players that are defending the attack. Game situations, such as; 1-on-1, 2-on-2 are classified as **EVEN-MAN OFFENSIVE ATTACKS**.

EVEN-MAN RULE: Goaltenders MUST begin outside the crease and hold their ground in the Ready (SET) Position when an **EVEN-MAN OFFENSIVE ATTACK** begins to develop during a game.

IMPORTANT NOTE: Goaltenders MUST always challenge the shooter during an **EVEN-MAN OFFENSIVE ATTACK**. By challenging in the Ready (SET) Position, goaltenders will automatically cut down the amount of open net available to a shooter that will try to use the defenseman as a screen. In addition, by challenging the play, goaltenders are in great position to reach a loose puck that is sliding through the defenseman's skates preventing a possible breakaway from developing.

2-on-1's - *Try Me!* Using the **ODD/EVEN** concept, *educated goaltenders* strive to allow 2-on-1 game situations to *come to them!*

While waiting for the puck carrier to close in on a 2-on-1, goaltenders will find most success by becoming prepared in the Ready (SET) Position at the top of the goal crease understanding that **the puck carrier is his/her responsibility**.

Facing a strong scoring chance such as this, goaltenders need to *out-wait* the shooter while reading the body language that the shooter is presenting. Most 2-on-1 scoring chances will entice shooters to attempt to pick the top corner on the short-side with a great snap or wrist shot!

Knowing that this is a favourite scoring shot for most shooters, *educated goaltenders* may take advantage of this knowledge by:

1. making the shooter think that the top corner has an opening on the short-side and taking it away by using a slight, quick positional shift to the short-side which may also force shooters to shoot wide missing the net completely
2. using the **NEW** Bradford's Goal Academy design save called the **HIGH-FIVE SAVE**

Knowing when the shot is about to take place is a great advantage for goaltenders. Goaltenders must be extremely conscious of any **quick release** shots that shooters may attack them with.

IMPORTANT NOTE: Goaltenders that position themselves correctly at the top of the crease during a 2-on-1 game situation (i.e., an **ODD-MAN OFFENSIVE ATTACK**) also have a realistic chance of making a *great save* by following any last second pass attempts across the slot. When a goaltender stops a tough 2-on-1 scoring chance, the great save provides his/her team with a huge, positive lift and may result in being the difference in a game.

GREAT GOALTENDERS make GREAT SAVES
at GREAT MOMENTS in a game!

3-on-2's - *I GOTCHA!* Comparable to 2-on-1 game situations, goaltenders must use the **ODD/EVEN** concept to establish proper positioning as the 3-on-2 game situation approaches. *Educated* goaltenders will usually see a 3-on-2 begin to develop near center ice. Goaltenders must use a Sideways Shuffle across the top of the crease to follow all puck movements. It is also very important for goaltenders to continually establish a Ready (SET) Position in order to be prepared for any quick release shots that may come through the defenseman's legs.

DECISION TIME: Once the opposition gains the blue line, the goaltender *reads the play* and determines which player on the 3-on-2 will become the *dangerous trailing player!*

It is at this moment when goaltenders must focus entirely on the *trailing player* that receives the pass. The other two players attacking on a 3-on-2 will drive hard to the net skating through the defensemen trying to create a screen for the *trailing player* to shoot through.

ATTENTION GOALTENDERS: When you see the pass going to the *trailing player,* you MUST take a strong step **OUT** to challenge the shooter as if it was a *breakaway!* You MUST follow any sideways (*east to west*) movement that the shooter may make while carrying the puck. Making a *GREAT SAVE* on a 3-on-2 is only **HALF** the battle! Due to the fact that there are two other opposition players circling around the crease area on a 3-on-2, it is extremely important for goaltenders to have great **Rebound Control!**

Coach Brent Bradford and Coach Vic LeMire state:

ONE SHOT - NO REBOUND!
(That is the WINNING WAY to play Goal!)

CHAPTER 26 - BREAKAWAYS - *Bring 'Em On!*

ATTENTION GOALTENDERS: Playing Breakaways effectively involves having a *specific attitude*! We cannot impress upon you enough that finding success when facing Breakaways begins and ends with a ... *"You can't beat me"* ... attitude!

All the statistics indicate that goaltenders are totally successful in nearly 7 out of every 10 Breakaway situations. That equates to 70% of the time! That is quite *significant*!

Within this important chapter, we will bring to light all the pertinent skills and very important mindsets that every *educated goaltender* is required to possess in order to be successful on stopping Breakaways during regular time and shootouts.

There are several required skills that every goaltender MUST learn and practice on a regular basis in order to *master the art* of stopping Breakaways. Effective goaltenders will:

1. begin by challenging out several feet on top of the goal crease
2. wait, wait, wait - patience must be maintained until the player crosses the **Breakaway Line**
3. skate backwards matching the player's speed
4. force the player to shoot or deke

It is up to the goaltender!
GOALTENDERS are in complete CONTROL!

CHALLENGING: It is extremely important for goaltenders to challenge out approximately three to four feet outside the top of the goal crease at the exact moment they realize that a Breakaway is about to take place. Goaltenders will **EXPLODE** out and *STOP* while a proper mindset is being quickly prepared which includes understanding that: **THE GOALTENDER IS IN CHARGE!**

Some game situations (e.g., Mini-Breakaways) restrict goaltenders from moving out of the goal crease very far because the player is already at the doorstep. It is crucial for goaltenders to always attempt to gain as much *ice territory* as possible before the Breakaway gets too involved.

The BREAKAWAY LINE: Wait, Wait, Wait! With more than 60-plus years of combined goaltending experience and research, Goaltending Coaches Brent Bradford and Vic LeMire have established the special *Breakaway Line* to play breakaways properly. Crossing this important imaginary line, which flows *east to west* across the top of the face-off circles, determines the actual *starting point* of the Breakaway for goaltenders. A goaltender **MUST** use the *Breakaway Line* to establish *proper timing* while following the player back to the net.

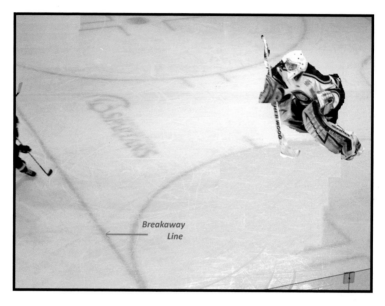

Breakaway
Line

MATCHING THE PLAYER'S SPEED: Goaltenders need this gained *ice territory*, described above, to begin playing the Breakaway similarly to how a defenseman plays a forward on a 1-on-1. Goaltenders must attempt to *match the player's skating speed* as the player approaches. If the player is skating toward the goaltender *FAST,* the goaltender skates backwards *FAST*. If the player skates in *SLOWLY,* the goaltender also skates backwards *SLOWLY*.

IMPORTANT NOTE #1: If the goaltender *waits too long* before he/she begins to skate backwards towards the net, the player will skate easily around him/her.

IMPORTANT NOTE #2: If the goaltender begins to skate backwards too soon, he/she will end up too deep in the net which will offer the player too much net to shoot at.

A Physical Fact occurs as the goaltender waits for the player to cross the **Breakaway Line** and begins to match the speed of the player.

PHYSICAL FACT: The large distance, that separates the goaltender from the player as the player crosses the **Breakaway Line,** will shrink quickly bringing the player very close to the goaltender. If timed correctly, the goaltender will be at the very top edge of the goal crease (great positioning) as the player is forced to make a decision on the Breakaway.

This properly timed backwards skating skill will provide the goaltender with plenty of momentum for continued backwards and/or sideways movement to follow the player as necessary.

Good "timing"

Bad "timing"

GOALTENDERS ARE IN CONTROL: All *elite* goaltenders have learned (or should have learned) the various techniques required to make shooters do exactly what goaltenders want them to do on Breakaways. If a goaltender simply sits back and waits for the player to do what the player wants to do on a Breakaway, then the goaltender has little or no time to figure the player out. This will leave the goaltender with a distinct disadvantage especially with higher skilled professional players.

MEMORABLE GOALTENDER HISTORY! It is easy for one to remember great NHL goaltenders such as **Tony Esposito** and **Roger Crozier** opening up a huge 5-hole for players to shoot at, tempting them only to close that gap in rapid-like fashion en route to making a great save!

POP QUIZ: Did the players *want* to shoot at that huge 5-hole, or ... did the great goaltenders **force the players** to shoot there?

CONSIDER THIS: How can a goaltender *trigger* the player to move to the goaltender's right side? YES, a simple, quick short side-step to the goaltender's left will FORCE the player to go in the other direction. Truthfully, the goaltender is actually **loading up** his/her left leg to push HARD back to the right post following the player as *planned* by the goaltender!

ATTENTION GOALTENDERS: It will take plenty of practice and experience for you to know exactly *when* to make this *fake*, but, do not let the player FAKE you out ... YOU FAKE him/her out first!

REMEMBER ... YOU are in CONTROL for success!

PLAYER'S OPTIONS: It is important to understand that there are merely three options that a player can choose to apply on a Breakaway. The player can:

1. DEKE
2. SHOOT
3. FAKE a shot and then DEKE

1. DEKE = FAKE: A player will *telegraph* that he/she is intending to try to DEKE a goaltender by approaching with his/her legs spread very wide apart. The player will also have the puck directly in front of him/herself. This posture provides the player with a great deal of **east to west** mobility and takes away from a shooting posture. **Experienced** and **educated** goaltenders will identify this leg posture developing as the player approaches the lower slot area.

IMPORTANT NOTE: *Goaltenders must NEVER fall for the first FAKE!* The actual *word* itself tells you that this first move is NOT the real move that the player is going to use! It is a FAKE ... so goaltenders should *NEVER FALL FOR IT!* The **intelligent, educated** goaltender will force the player to believe that he/she has fallen for the DEKE by making a slight move in the wrong direction. This can be a:

1. slight step sideways
2. a slight body/weight shift
3. a quick head bob

Any of these goaltender **FAKES** will force the player to believe that he/she has succeeded in making the goaltender fall for the **DEKE!**

ATTENTION GOALTENDERS: This quick move must be applied at exactly the *correct time* in order to be effective. This exact moment is just before the player makes his/her final decision to DEKE the goaltender. The *old school theory* of *goaltenders not making the first move* no longer has merit as modern day goaltenders are taught to take control of Breakaways. Even the goaltender's initial positioning can force the player to make a decision to *Shoot* or to *Deke*!

What should properly happen is that the **elite** goaltender will give a FAKE of his/her own making the player believe that he/she fooled the goaltender! This fake in reverse allows the **goaltender** to be **IN CHARGE** of the play. The goaltender has forced the player to go around and the goaltender now knows which side the player is moving to.

IN OTHER WORDS: It is as if the goaltender has become a *card dealer* and the goaltender has cunningly dealt the losing cards to the shooter. The goaltender is forcing the player to play those losing cards. The goaltender must now analyze the player to figure out if the player is going to perform one of the many available options, such as:

1. tap the puck through the 5-hole
2. carry the puck around the goaltender to the far post and shoot low
3. flip the puck high into the top corner of the net

IMPORTANT NOTE: It is imperative for goaltenders to understand that different Breakaway procedures should be implemented whether the shooter is left-handed or right-handed.

One of the very first observations that a goaltender must figure out is ... *is the player right-handed or left-handed?* This will determine if a Poke Check (see Chapter 10) may be the best save selection to use on the Breakaway.

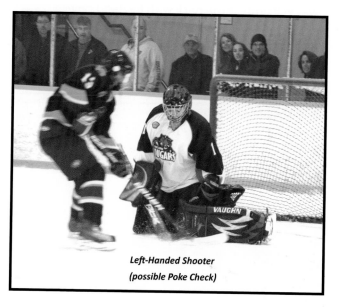

Left-Handed Shooter
(possible Poke Check)

IMPORTANT NOTE FOR GOALTENDERS THAT CATCH WITH THE LEFT HAND: *LEFT-HANDED PLAYERS* - Experienced goaltenders that catch with the left hand may use an explosive *Poke Check* on a *left-handed player* coming in on a Breakaway if the player is approaching from:

1. directly down the middle of the ice surface
2. the left-wing position and cutting in

IMPORTANT NOTE FOR GOALTENDERS THAT CATCH WITH THE RIGHT HAND: *RIGHT-HANDED PLAYERS* - Experienced goaltenders that catch with the right hand may use an explosive *Poke Check* on a *right-handed player* coming in on a Breakaway if the player is approaching from:

1. directly down the middle of the ice surface
2. the right-wing position cutting in

IMPORTANT NOTE: *Left-handed* goaltenders should never attempt to Poke Check a left-handed player that is approaching from the right-wing position. The goaltender's stick cannot reach the puck, as the left-handed player will protect the puck with his/her body.

IMPORTANT NOTE: *Right-handed* goaltenders should never attempt to Poke Check a right-handed player that is approaching from the left-wing position. The goaltender's stick cannot reach the puck, as the right-handed player will protect the puck with his/her body.

RIGHT-HANDED GOALTENDERS: A *Sweep Check*, with the full length of the stick, may be effective from time to time when *left-handed players* approach from the left wing.

Very good "timing"

LEFT-HANDED GOALTENDERS: Experienced left-handed goaltenders may use an explosive Poke Check on a *right-handed player* coming in on a Breakaway if the player is approaching on his/her backhand from the left-wing ONLY!

RIGHT-HANDED GOALTENDERS: Experienced right-handed goaltenders may use an explosive Poke Check on a *left-handed player* coming in on a Breakaway if the player is approaching on his/her backhand from the right-wing ONLY!

LEFT-HANDED GOALTENDERS: A *sweep-check*, with the full length of the stick, may be effective from time to time when *right-handed players* approach from the right wing.

ATTENTION GOALTENDERS: DO NOT attempt either a Poke Check or a Sweep Check if the player is approaching from directly down the *middle of the ice surface.*

In addition to using the Poke Check *weapon* on Breakaways, advanced goaltenders will be able to add **FAKE POKE CHECKS** to their arsenal. **FAKE POKE CHECKS** are just as effective as the real thing! Using a **FAKE POKE CHECK** will cause the player to pull up short and try to score on the short-side. This will be an easy save for the goaltender to make because of the backwards skating momentum that has already been built up. The goaltender will drive across to the short-side protecting all of the lower part of the net while looking for any possibility of a high level shot.

2. SHOT: As with DEKES, the goaltender MUST also be IN CHARGE of the Breakaway when a player is in a shooting position. The goaltender will recognize that the player's legs are very close together and the puck is positioned to the side of the player.

The success of a player that shoots on a breakaway is determined completely by the *release speed* of the shot! A player with a very quick release and professional accuracy makes it extremely difficult for the goaltender to stop the puck.

To maximize the goaltender's success, proper positioning at the top of the goal crease makes the player have to hit a very small target in one of the four corners of the net or the 5-hole. As the player releases the shot, it is the goaltender's intuition and reflexes that allow for an explosive movement towards the spot that the goaltender has chosen to give to the player.

Giving up too much net space will make stopping a quick release shot virtually impossible. With experience and lots of practice, goaltenders will learn to *read the player's signals* on a shot and great saves will be the result.

ATTENTION GOALTENDERS: One of the best Breakaway Saves for a goaltender to make is inviting a huge 5-hole for the player to shoot at, only to *close the trap* with an explosive drop to the knees.

3. FAKE SHOT THEN A DEKE : The third Breakaway option, that a player may use, presents its own set of strategies necessary for the goaltender to find success.

The goaltender can FORCE the player to try to go around him/her (i.e., DEKE) in the direction that the goaltender chooses by making an initial quick FAKE moving slightly to the *long- side* then by exploding back to the *near-side* post. This technique **MUST be used** *BEFORE* the player applies his/her *(fake)* release of the shot.

The goaltender must also be fully prepared and well-positioned with his/her goal stick blade and ready to protect the very vulnerable 5-hole as the goaltender *opens up* to move across the crease.

IMPORTANT RULE: It is absolutely **MANDATORY** that the goaltender always follows the ***path of the puck*** with the blade of the goal stick! Although the goaltender may be exploding his/her leg pad across the ice to reach the far post, it is the positioning of the goal stick blade that will protect against the very clever **TAP-IN** manoeuvre between the open legs (i.e., 5-hole).

TWO-MAN BREAKAWAY: *Yes … It Is Time To Shine!* Every so often, a game situation occurs when a Two-Man Breakaway ascends down on a goaltender. Although this may appear as a totally unstoppable play, it actually is somewhat easier to stop than a single player breakaway.

WHY? The puck-carrier is under intense pressure to make the correct play without a mistake and, as such, the player most often will pass the puck at the last moment.

Goaltenders may play the Two-Man Breakaway in two ways:

✓ prepare to drive across the crease down low at the last moment to follow the pass to the open player
✓ cheat across slightly (i.e., FAKE) before the pass occurs causing the player to shoot the puck at the short-side … the goaltender may force

the player into shooting short-side and then can take that part of the net away making a **GREAT SAVE!**

A Statement from Coach Brent Bradford and Coach Vic LeMire:

A BREAKAWAY is the most exciting play in ALL sports.
Master the skill of stopping breakaways …
and you will be the star of many games!

A Bradford/LeMire Homework Assignment

Take your parents/guardians to a local Junior A, Major Junior, College, or University Hockey game and sit behind the goal. Study what the goaltender is doing well. Write down five key areas of the goaltender's game that you believe will help him/her reach professional hockey (e.g., communication, puck-handling, positioning, rebound control, confidence, overall hockey sense, etc.). After you have made your list of five areas, describe, in detail, why you believe each area is important to a goaltender's overall success?

PART SIX

CAREER DEVELOPMENT

CHAPTER 27 - CLUB-LEVEL HOCKEY

There are two main reasons why a goaltender plays Club-Level Hockey.

1. He/she chooses to on his/her own because reaching Advanced-Level Hockey may not be a top priority for him/her
2. He/she has not yet been recognized as an *Elite-Level* goaltender by his/her specific Hockey Organization due to lack of various important goaltender skills required to compete successfully at an elite level

Our focus will remain on the second reason throughout this chapter. After all, goaltenders that are reading this book must have **hockey** written down near the top of their priority list after **family** and **school!**

Goaltenders that are sent down to Club-Level Hockey, after trying out for *Elite-Level* hockey teams, MUST maintain a high level of determination in order to prove to those *Elite-Level* evaluators and coaches that they were wrong!

Playing Club-Level Hockey provides goaltenders with some hidden benefits that should be taken advantage of throughout the hockey season. Benefits include:

1. being able to practice puck-handling skills during game action because the play is a bit slower
2. being able to practice communication skills with teammates and coaches without worrying too much about incorrect decisions
3. being able to be a team leader both on and off the ice which would normally create more nervousness at higher levels of hockey
4. being able to help the coaches design goaltender-specific drills during practice (most coaches at Club-Level Hockey appreciate new ideas, drills, and strategies as they are learning as well)

Based upon personal experiences, goaltenders that have been asked to play Club-Level Hockey are usually very disappointed at first. However, when they observe the fact that they can be team leaders and work on individual skills in a less threatening environment than at Elite-Level Hockey, they begin to show signs of improvement both skill-wise and confident-wise.

ATTENTION GOALTENDERS: If your goal is to reach Elite-Level Hockey, then make every single practice, game, and off-ice team activity count so that you enhance your overall hockey and goaltending skills that will be required for next season's tryout camp!

If you sit and pout over your self-proclaimed unfair situation and complain all season without striving to improve your skills, you will undoubtedly find yourself back where you presently are next season!

REMEMBER: Your teammates deserve your best efforts every practice, game, and off-ice team activity!

IMPORTANT NOTE: Complaining will not help you gain friends on your team. Complaining will only help turn your teammates against you. In fact, some of your teammates may believe they are playing at a high-level of hockey; their hockey aspirations may not be the same as your aspirations.

ATTENTION GOALTENDERS: You need to ask yourself this loaded question: *What do I need to do to reach Elite-Level Hockey?* If Elite-Level Hockey is your main goal, then reach it! Work hard, work hard, and work hard ... and *do not complain* when you are playing Club-Level Hockey. Complaining will get you absolutely nowhere fast!

CHAPTER 28 - ELITE ATOM/PEEWEE HOCKEY

IMPORTANT NOTE: This chapter is aimed directly toward goaltenders that truly want to be selected as the *elite* goaltenders in their specific Hockey Organization by dedicating themselves to hours of training, practising, and studying the Game of Hockey. Being selected to play at the top levels of Atom and/or Peewee hockey during the early years of a goaltender's career can be important when it comes to:

1. Ice-Time Opportunities
2. Quality of Shots
3. Exposure

1. Ice-Time Opportunities: Goaltenders that are part of the top Atom and/or top Peewee Hockey Teams generally are provided with a busier schedule throughout the hockey season. They will have many more games and practices than teams at lower tiers. This provides goaltenders with a rich amount of practice times and game experiences allowing individual and team skill development to occur at a potentially more rapid pace.

Goaltenders that take advantage of the high number of ice-time practices and games will continue to progress and, most notably, should be able to remain at the top level of hockey throughout their Minor Hockey careers.

ATTENTION *ELITE* GOALTENDERS: Take full advantage of all the time on the ice you are provided with so that you can fine tune the skills that are required to reach the next level of hockey and remember ...

1. Do not be lazy in the drills!
2. NEVER forget how much work it took both on and off the ice to make the TOP team!
3. It will take even more hard work to stay at the TOP level!

2. Shot Quality: It should be understood that top teams have top players! It is these top players that will play major roles in the development of *elite* goaltenders. During practices, these players will be consistently shooting on the goaltenders with intentions of scoring. What better training could a goaltender ask for?

Goaltenders need to put forth 100% effort during practices so that when it is time to perform in a game, the skills have been practised and properly developed! Goaltender skills that should be worked on throughout every single practice are (see the specific chapters regarding the following list):

➢ Goaltender-Specific Skating
➢ Puck-Handling
➢ Angles and Positioning
➢ Rebound Control
➢ Communication
➢ Understanding the Coach's Game Plan

3. Exposure: Top Atom and/or Peewee Hockey Teams play all other **Elite-Level** teams in major tournaments all over the Nation! It is at these elite-level tournaments where hockey scouts gather to assess some of the most talented young goaltenders. Gaining a roster spot on a top Atom and/or a top Peewee Hockey Team provides a very valuable hockey career opportunity as this selection puts goaltenders in front of these hockey scouts.

The Stage Can Be Set! It is at these tournaments when young goaltenders have opportunities to **shine in the nets** and **play their absolute best** so that hockey scouts begin to take notice and decide to follow them along as the goaltenders enter Bantam "AAA" Hockey.

ATTENTION GOALTENDERS: Being selected to the top Atom and/or top Peewee Hockey Team in your Hockey Organization needs to be your main goal! Reaching this level of hockey is the first step to becoming an **elite** goaltender.

It Is Not The End Of The World! Every hockey season, many goaltenders are assigned to lower tiers after being unsuccessful at the highest-tier team tryouts. It is important for these goaltenders to understand that their hockey aspirations are not over! According to Roy Henderson of Global Sports Scouting Inc. (globalsportscamp.com), **"Players should always remember that it is not a race!"**

Being assigned to a different tier only means that at this point in their young goaltending careers, they are not yet viewed as one of the **elite** goaltenders in the Hockey Organization.

Being re-assigned after the team tryouts should help goaltenders heighten their intrinsic motivation in order to overcome this adversity. They should become motivated to **get back to work** and continue developing the skills that are required to become **elite** goaltenders so they are successful in being selected to the top team the following season!

ATTENTION *ELITE* GOALTENDERS: It is important to understand that there are *MANY* goaltenders that are playing at lower tiers of hockey than you this season! They are **eager to take your spot away** from you next season!

What is it going to take for you to keep your spot on the ELITE-LEVEL hockey team?

The answer is for you to figure out before it is too late!

CHAPTER 29 - BANTAM AAA HOCKEY

ATTENTION GOALTENDERS: Although *EVERY* year of hockey is an important year, graduating into the BANTAM level is when you truly begin to showcase your skills! It is at this BANTAM age bracket that all the serious scouting and recruitment begins for you. Whether it is a Junior "A" Program in your area or a High School Varsity Team in your future ... now is the age as a *Bantam Goaltender* that you need to produce *exceptional* game performances in front of all the recruiters that are scouting you.

There are TWO extremely important showcase platforms that will occur during your Bantam years of hockey. They are TOURNAMENTS and PLAYOFFS!

Realize that there are so very many hockey teams all over the nation and as such Junior and College Scouts are physically unable to cover every game. These important *Scouts* migrate in mass to almost every Bantam Tournament and Playoff match-up hoping to get a read on the best *Prospects* available.

WILL YOU BE PREPARED? It makes complete sense for YOU to be totally prepared both mentally and physically to be recognized as the *Most Valuable Player* (MVP) of as many tournament and/or playoff games as you can. NOW is the time to play *"Lights Out"* goaltending!

IMPORTANT: Although playing at the AAA Level is extremely valuable as a Bantam goaltender, it is NOT a guarantee that this will move you up the recruitment ladder. Goaltenders, like every other athlete, grow and mature at very different ages. Those goaltenders that maintain a serious, dedicated work ethic will eventually find their moment to shine in the eyes of the hockey recruiters.

The *BANTAM DRAFT* is the first report card of your goaltending skills. Major Junior Hockey Teams gather each year with their scouts striving to identify all the *elite* goaltenders playing in their recruitment zones. Being drafted is an honour. Becoming a *first* or *second round draft pick* will signify that the team that drafts you is showing a very serious interest in having you become a member of their organization one day soon.

If you become a first or second round draft pick, this tells you that you are being considered as one of the BEST goaltenders in the world at your age! Congratulations! You have now put the wheels in motion to possibly become a dominant goaltender in Major Junior "A" Hockey.

ATTENTION GOALTENDERS: However, being drafted in the third, fourth or later rounds of the Major Junior Bantam Draft should be notification to you that you are a good, recognizable goaltender for your age. This should also indicate to you that you are *NOT* yet the *cream of the crop*. Being drafted in these later rounds or *NOT* being drafted at all *could also be a blessing* to you as this should tell you that you should *NOT YET* make the decision to become a Major Junior "A" goaltender. You would be very wise to keep on working hard by keeping your options open and staying eligible for a possible NCAA Hockey Scholarship in a few years!

If you are in this group of late drafted or non-drafted goaltenders, DO NOT play a single game of Major Junior "A" Hockey as playing even one game may cost you NCAA Hockey Scholarship eligibility! **BE AWARE**, as Major Junior Hockey Teams may create intense pressure on you and your family to sign a contract with them and get you to play one or two games. You must know that this may disqualify you from ever receiving a NCAA Hockey Scholarship in the future! Roy Henderson from Global Sports Scouting Inc. (globalsportscamp.com) wisely states, *"Make sure you do your research."*

As you grow and develop your skills through your teenage years you will be much better positioned to eventually make that *INFORMED* decision to either sign with a Major Junior "A" Hockey Team or accept a NCAA Hockey Scholarship. How awesome would it be to be in a position to have several options to choose from?

Realize that being drafted also signifies that you are now confined to play Major Junior "A" Hockey ONLY for the team that has drafted you (unless they trade your playing rights to another Major Junior "A" Hockey Team). As a drafted goaltender, you have no say as to which Major Junior "A" Hockey Team you can play for. This may or may not be an issue for you depending on the relationship you develop with that organization.

IN CONCLUSION: *Special Friend of ours* and Legendary Scout and founder of Global Sports Scouting Inc. (globalsportscamps.com), Roy Henderson definitely states it best:

"The best advice I can give a future player is: There is one guarantee in hockey and that is, ***there is no guarantee***! Try not to put all your ***eggs in one basket***. It is always best to have a backup plan. Many of those promises that are made in hockey do not seem to happen. It is our hope, that regardless of where you are with your hockey career, you will remember the importance of a good education. Strive to play at the highest possible level. Keep in mind, playing hockey should always be ***fun***. ***Players should always remember that it is not a race!*** Take your time and do it right. Make sure you do your research! It takes good information to make good decisions. The order should be as follows: ***family, school and then hockey***. Try not to mix these up and you should be fine. Have a good season and make good decisions. We hope to see you in either: Burnaby, Chicago, or Las Vegas Camps!"

/ Roy Henderson

CHAPTER 30 - MIDGET AAA/HIGH SCHOOL HOCKEY

Once goaltenders graduate from Bantam-Level Hockey, various playing opportunities may become available to them such as:

➤ Midget Hockey
➤ High School Hockey
➤ Junior "B" Hockey
➤ Junior "A" Hockey
➤ Major Junior "A" Hockey

Some very important *family decisions* need to be made at this time in an aspiring *elite* goaltender's life. Questions that aspiring *elite* goaltenders need to answer are:

✓ Am I ready to leave home to play hockey and go to a new high school to graduate?
✓ Which hockey program and specific Coaching Staffs should I be searching for?
✓ How mature and independent am I at this age (can I co-exist with older athletes)?
✓ Do I want to forgo any potential future NCAA opportunities and *put all my eggs in one basket* by agreeing to sign with a Major Junior "A" Hockey Organization at this young age?

IMPORTANT NOTE #1: If the (Family) answer to any of these questions is NO, then the only place goaltenders should be aiming to play for is their local Midget or High School Hockey Team!

It is important to play for the local Midget AAA Hockey Team or the equivalent Varsity High School Hockey Team if the ultimate goal is to play Junior "A" Hockey in a season or two; otherwise, playing Midget AA, Midget B, or Junior Varsity is the next best level of opportunity.

IMPORTANT NOTE #2: If the (Family) answer to some of these questions is YES, then the direction that hockey goaltenders need to research does change dramatically!

With the assistance of *special knowledge* from various trusted hockey coaches and scouts, goaltenders may want to relocate their lives and hockey careers to play for a well-known and respected Junior "B", Junior "A", or Major Junior "A" Hockey Organization at this age.

There are many advantages, for goaltenders that are Midget-age, to be playing Junior Hockey. Hockey Scouts pay extra attention to these younger (blue chip) athletes that can compete with confidence and great results at this *Elite Level*.

BE AWARE: There are also some risks involved when playing in advanced leagues where players are older and stronger. If a young goaltender's skills are not developed enough to provide a reasonable chance of showcasing advanced talent, then, many scouts may pre-judge his/her ultimate potential incorrectly and this may disrupt his/her chances for advancement in the future.

A Bradford/LeMire Homework Assignment

After watching and studying an NHL hockey game, record a television interview of an NHL goaltender following the game (e.g., win, loss, shutout). Type out the interview (ask your parent/guardian to help with the typing if that is needed). Study what types of questions were asked and what the goaltender said well and what you believe was not stated well. Why do you think the goaltender chose to answer certain questions in a specific manner? Do you believe the goaltender was respectful to: teammates, opposing players, referees, etc.? Write down how you would have responded differently to certain questions.

CHAPTER 31 - JUNIOR "B" HOCKEY

Unknown to most hockey families, there are many high caliber Junior "B" Hockey Leagues available throughout North America. The Junior "B" Hockey experience may be the perfect **jumping stone** from Minor Hockey to Junior "A" Hockey!

Goaltenders that have already played one year of Midget or Varsity High School Hockey may discover that playing one year of Junior "B" Hockey will prepare them nicely with more competition than repeating a second year of Midget or Varsity High School Hockey.

There are many Junior "B" Hockey Leagues that have produced goaltenders strong enough to receive NCAA Hockey Scholarships directly without having to play a year or two of Junior "A" Hockey elsewhere. These stronger Junior "B" Hockey Leagues are usually located in smaller hockey markets where *elite* players choose to remain closer to home to finish their high school education.

HOMEWORK ASSIGNMENT: Research the many Junior "B" Hockey Leagues and pay attention to specific team's motives toward developing top quality goaltenders en route to higher levels of hockey.

ATTENTION GOALTENDERS: One other advantage for playing at least one year of Junior "B" Hockey is to eliminate the *import* classification you may be labeled with. Once you have finished playing Minor Hockey and should you choose to move to a different Province or State to play Junior Hockey, you will then be classified as an *import* goaltender!

This **import** status may become a harmful classification on your resume because Junior "A" Hockey Teams are limited to the total number of import players they can have on their teams.

By playing one season of Junior "B" Hockey in the Province or State that you wish to eventually play Junior "A" Hockey in will convert your *import* status to a more desirable *non-import* status the following year. This will provide you with a greater opportunity to make the Junior "A" Hockey Team you are striving to make!

CHAPTER 32 - JUNIOR "A" HOCKEY

ATTENTION GOALTENDERS: Becoming a Junior "A" Hockey player is the culmination and reward for every single early morning Minor Hockey practice that you and your whole family endured over many years. Playing Junior "A" Hockey symbolizes a variety of things to each goaltender that is fortunate enough to graduate from the Minor Hockey System.

Junior "A" Hockey - *What To Expect*

➢ Most reputable Junior "A" Hockey Teams provide goaltender equipment including sticks. This equates to an enormous saving for families with goaltenders that, for so many years, have contributed vast sums of money for such expensive equipment.
➢ Most often, playing Junior "A" Hockey means that the goaltender must move away from home for the first time in his/her life. Sometimes it is just across town, but, more often than not, it is in a different *city* or even a different *province* or *country*!
➢ The goaltender will be introduced to a local, welcoming family called a **Billet Family**. Many great life-long relationships are formed through *Billet Families*. Goaltenders will usually become a *hero* to the children and to the billet Mother and Father.

These changes in a goaltender's life will present many special moments as well as some common challenges that are required to be overcome in order to establish a great learning atmosphere for:

1. school studies
2. hockey growth
3. social wellness
4. maturity, independence, and responsibility

Complete **RESPECT** toward the **Billet Family** MUST be a primary concern during the goaltender's daily activities. There are several items that must be adhered to when residing in a **Billet Family's Home.**

1. It is imperative to understand completely that members of the *Billet Family* are NOT meant to be your personal maids!
2. It is important to maintain a clean and tidy bedroom.

3. Proper bedtime hours (which are set by the team and/or the *Billet Family*) must be adhered to for everyone's benefit, especially for your benefit (e.g., enough sleep in order to perform at a top level).
4. Headphones must be used to play your own personal music selections unless one of your family members is joining in on your listening amusement (if this is the case, the music should not be too loud). Others in the household may be studying, working, practicing an instrument, or carrying on a conversation (loud music is both distracting and disrespectful toward other family members).
5. Regular communications should be made with your family back home. No long distance phone calls should be charged to the *Billet Family*.
6. It is essential for goaltenders to assist in all the household chores (e.g., dishes, house cleaning, laundry, and trash removal).
7. Regular, sincere attention and interest in the billet children's activities and schoolwork MUST be demonstrated.
8. Goaltenders should NEVER bring friends back to the billet home without the family's approval.
9. Asking permission for food and/or drinks consistently indicates a high amount of respect toward the *billet family*.
10. There should be absolutely NO smoking, alcohol, or drug use in the billet home! Absolutely none!

IMPORTANT NOTE: Playing Junior "A" Hockey means that you will be fully associated with teammates ranging from fifteen to twenty years old. You face many decisions that will have such an important effect on your young life as an independent young athlete. Quite often, there may be high school parties or after game celebrations that may involve the presence of alcohol and/or drugs. Make the decision to leave these potential celebrations WITHOUT accepting a ride from anyone who is under the influence of alcohol and/or drugs!

WHAT TO DO IN THIS SITUATION?

1. take a cab ride home
2. contact your *Billet Family* for a ride home
3. contact one of your coaches for a ride home

MAINTAINING SCHOOL GRADES: Establishing proper daily study sessions in order to maintain the highest possible Grade Point Average (GPA) will keep you eligible for an NCAA Hockey Scholarship. It may be difficult to decide to pass on a team card-playing event, (e.g., on the bus ride or at a teammates home) but, you MUST keep your priorities straight! Nobody will be babysitting you! It will be your responsibility to make mature, sometimes life-saving decisions, during your Junior "A" Hockey career! You will NOT earn an NCAA Hockey Scholarship for being the greatest *Poker Player* on the team!

JUNIOR "A" HOCKEY ... NOT MINOR HOCKEY

ATTENTION GOALTENDERS: It will become evident that you are no longer in Minor Hockey from the very first moment you step onto the ice as a Junior "A" Hockey goaltender. Many of the changes you will be exposed to as you begin a Junior "A" Hockey career are listed below.

1. Equal ice time *will NOT be guaranteed*. As a matter of fact, it *is guaranteed* that you will NOT get equal ice time. You must be prepared to deal with that by working even harder for the ice time you deserve.
2. Meeting **ALL** scheduled team events (e.g., practice times, game times, and bus departures) ON TIME (even early) is your responsibility.
3. Your nutritional intake and body fitness will be closely monitored.
4. Your school grades will be monitored and your hockey playing time will be dealt with accordingly.
5. Off-ice workouts become mandatory.
6. Coaches will be more intense and demanding of individual performances.
7. You must learn how to accept and deal with personal assessments (often times in front of teammates) despite how demanding and/or embarrassing they may be.
8. Your on-ice work ethic will be assessed after each practice and each game.
9. Coaches DO NOT EVER want to hear from your parents about any hockey-related subject. They only want to hear from YOU!
10. Goaltenders are subject to trades or dismissal from the teams without input or consideration for their individual needs.

CHAPTER 33 - MAJOR JUNIOR "A" HOCKEY

It is important to understand completely all the particular differences between playing Junior "A" Hockey and playing MAJOR Junior "A" Hockey.

BECOME EDUCATED! Anyone who decides to play a single game or attend the Main Training Camp of a Major Junior "A" Hockey Team shall do so with full understanding that they may immediately become ineligible to receive an NCAA Hockey Scholarship! It is worth researching the new rules surrounding this point from time to time.

This is a very serious decision that must be made with complete consultation and understanding
by one's parents and other influential hockey people
in the community.

Playing for a Major Junior "A" Hockey Organization has a tremendous amount of great benefits, including:

1. A high majority of **NHL Draft Picks** come from the various Major Junior "A" Hockey Teams.
2. An extremely high level of **Professional Coaching** exists.
3. There is a rich amount of exposure to **Professional Scouts**.
4. A very intensive hockey schedule provides a large number of games throughout the season.
5. Becoming a TOP first or second round NHL Draft Pick practically insures the possibility of signing a **Professional Hockey Contract**.
6. A great amount of ice time occurs as players are on the ice virtually every day.
7. An **Education Package** is available with most Major Junior "A" Hockey Organizations (which provides one year of paid tuition to a Canadian University or College for each completed year of playing Major Junior "A" Hockey - it is worth researching on your own the rules concerning this item from time to time as they may amended).
8. A **Hockey Career** becomes the emphasis!
9. **Billet Families** become great life-long friends.

BE PREPARED! Within the Major Junior "A" Hockey System, there are several serious drawbacks that may or may not affect goaltenders as follows:

1. Education is no longer the priority although each goaltender is encouraged to do his/her best with the limited study time available to him/her. Due to the intense travel schedule on long bus trips, very little time is scheduled for studying or completing school assignments. Generally the bus trips are comprised of long card games (which are personal decisions) or simply needed sleep between cities.
2. Negotiated *Educational Packages*, discussed above, may have a limited list of Canadian Colleges or Canadian Universities to choose from (it is worth researching on your own the rules concerning this item from time to time as they may amended).
3. Goaltenders are subject to *trades* or *dismissal* from the teams without input or consideration for their personal needs.

IMPORTANT NOTE: If one is drafted in the lower rounds of the NHL Draft or simply not drafted at all, (which happens to many goaltenders each year) and he/she does not continue a Semi-Professional Hockey Career, he/she is then left to enter the *real work force*.

Often one enters the work force with minimal working skills or education. At this time, one may also begin attending a Canadian University or College (which can provide him/her with an extended hockey career in very talented leagues) by exercising a *Major Junior "A" Hockey Education Package*.

ATTENTION PARENTS/GUARDIANS: Do your homework when helping your goaltender through life-altering hockey decisions. **BE INFORMED!**

Did You Know …

Ken Dryden chose to pursue a Bachelor of Arts Degree at Cornell University, where he also played hockey until his graduation in 1969 rather than play in Montreal.

Every young goaltender dreams about playing in the NHL. That dream just might come true for you. However, it is important to note that only a small number of goaltenders will ever make it to the NHL. Reaching that dream is so very difficult, but with a lot of **hard work** and many **great performances**, your path to the TOP may be just ahead of you!

That is why:
HOCKEY + EDUCATION = ENDLESS OPPORTUNITIES

One of the absolute *GREATEST* paths that goaltenders can *MAP OUT* is to earn a Full Athletic Hockey Scholarship to an NCAA School. Also, partial scholarships are available as you begin your **Freshman** and **Sophomore** years at various Colleges/Universities. The partial scholarships may progress into full scholarships during your **Junior** and **Senior** years on campus if your grades and hockey skills evolve to the highest standards.

> *"Although playing Junior "A" Hockey will provide many great memories for goaltenders …*
> *I believe there is NO comparison to the four years that one will spend playing for an NCAA University/College Hockey Team!"*
> */Coach Vic LeMire*

PERSONAL EXPERIENCE (Coach Vic LeMire): I will speak of this chapter with such personal experience as a former NCAA goaltender. I tell you enthusiastically that playing University/College Hockey will be the absolute **BEST FOUR YEARS** of your life if you are fortunate enough to earn a hockey scholarship!

Obtaining a Full Athletic Hockey Scholarship is a realistic opportunity for the many goaltenders competing in today's Minor and Junior Hockey systems. Staying eligible by having a dominating Junior "A" or High School Hockey career along with producing a strong Grade Point Average (GPA) with your high school grades will put you in front of the eager eyes of **ALL** the NCAA recruiters.

IMPORTANT NOTE: It is NOT mandatory to have to earn an NCAA Hockey Scholarship directly after a goaltender has completed his/her senior year of high school. As a matter of fact, it may be to the goaltender's benefit to continue to play Junior "A Hockey through his/her 19 or 20 year old hockey season instead.

The NCAA Hockey Program is an extremely high calibre league comprised of exceptionally talented young men/women who are big and strong athletes. Young 17 or 18 year olds, who join that league, may be required to watch most of the games from the bench during their first year in order to enhance their individual skills and to grow stronger.

ATTENTION GOALTENDERS: Developing your skills along with your strength and conditioning for a couple more years in Junior "A" Hockey is highly recommended in order to become fully prepared for a University/College Hockey career. It is critical for goaltenders to revisit the comments of one of the most reputable hockey scouts, Roy Henderson of Global Sports Scouting Inc.,

"It's important to understand that it's NOT a race!"

ATTENTION GOALTENDERS: If NCAA recruiters and coaches are displaying an interest in you as a 17 or 18 year old goaltender, they most certainly will be *pounding down your door* when you are playing Junior "A" Hockey as a 19 or 20 year old. By extending a Junior "A" Hockey career, goaltenders will discover many more NCAA schools striving to recruit them.

ARE YOU AWARE? Goaltenders are eligible to accept up to five different *fly-downs* to look over each school's program PRIOR to making a final decision (it is worth researching on your own the rules concerning this item from time to time as they may amended).

ATTENTION GOALTENDERS: You are in charge of the choice when it comes to deciding on a school! This will be a great moment in your life. You will arrive at University/College as an excited teenager and return after four years as a properly educated strong, young MAN!

A STATEMENT BASED ON PERSONAL EXPERIENCE:

"Goaltenders ...
this will be the BEST four years of your life!"

/Coach Vic LeMire

IMPORTANT NOTE: While attending University/College, your dream of one day playing in the NHL is still very plausible. Many educated goaltenders do sign *lucrative Free Agent NHL Contracts*. The most important aspect of playing University/College Hockey is:

➢ Should the illusive NHL path you once hoped for not happen, you have earned a **STRONG education** which will set you up for a very good job position.

This is NOT the case if a goaltender decided to play Major Junior "A" Hockey (instead of NCAA) and fails to reach Professional and/or Canadian University Hockey! Most often, in this case, goaltenders are left with little or no higher education and minimal job skills!

Coach Brent Bradford and Coach Vic LeMire highly recommend …
that you make ALL your choices only AFTER you and your family have become totally informed of the
advantages and disadvantages of playing
Major Junior "A" Hockey versus NCAA University/College Hockey!

Do your homework so you make the most educated decision either way!

CHAPTER 35 - CANADIAN UNIVERSITY/COLLEGE HOCKEY

At the end of a goaltender's Junior "A" or Major Junior "A" Hockey career (or in some instances, after Junior "B", Midget, or High School Hockey), both male and female goaltenders will have some extremely important questions to answer if a professional hockey opportunity is not expected in the *immediate* future.

A few of these questions include:

1. Do you want your competitive hockey career to be over?
2. Do you want to enter the work force with, for the most part, limited skills and limited education because you have spent the last few years concentrating solely on building a hockey career?
3. Is there a professional occupation you want to strive for (e.g., technology, business, education, law, medicine, etc.) that will require a University or College Degree?

The answers to these simple questions can be difficult once goaltenders turn 21 years old. We stress the importance of a quality education so that goaltenders can experience a financially and emotionally stable lifestyle after a competitive hockey career is complete.

CANADIAN UNIVERSITY/COLLEGE HOCKEY: There is no better way to acquire a quality education than to play University or College Hockey in Canada while your burning desire to compete still exists as you enter your early 20's.

The most notable Canadian University Hockey League is the Canadian Inter-University Sport (CIS). It has been commonly stated that the CIS is arguably the most underrated league in North America. For instance, the majority of players competing in CIS Men's Hockey include ex-top Junior "A" players and Major Junior "A" players.

This talent-filled hockey league offers goaltenders with opportunities to:

1. compete at an extremely high level of hockey
2. continue developing goaltender skills required to take a forward step into Professional Hockey
3. play on a team with high level coaching
4. be part of the University sports scene

5. attain a quality education from a prestigious Canadian University

At the end of a CIS career, goaltenders will again find themselves with some major questions to answer. After attaining a **quality education** at University and being part of a talent-filled hockey league, a few of these questions include:

1. Do you want your competitive hockey career to be over?
2. Are you ready to step away from competitive hockey so that you can enter the work force with a **solid education in your back pocket**?

FOLLOWING A CIS HOCKEY CAREER: There are a few basic options that the majority of goaltenders take after their CIS hockey careers are complete:

1. many goaltenders strive to enter **Professional Hockey** and are successful due to the skills that were developed throughout their time in the CIS
2. some goaltenders decide to enter the work force using their **education** as a starting point
3. some goaltenders continue to enrol in **University Courses** in order to attain even higher levels of education (e.g., Masters Degree, Doctor of Philosophy Degree)

ATTENTION GOALTENDERS: Whatever path you choose to take after your CIS Hockey career is complete, one thing needs to be clear, **No one can ever take away the education you earned during your years of attending Canadian University while playing hockey!**

A Statement from Coach Brent Bradford ...

"Playing hockey for the University of Alberta Golden Bears in the CIS offered me many life-altering experiences. I was able to compete alongside top-notch goaltender partners and high-caliber teammates. Being part of the 1999 CIAU (now known as the CIS) National Championship Hockey Team demonstrated to me what it takes for a team to complete its mission. In addition to being part of such a hard working hockey team, I was able to land a full-time teaching job only one month after completing a Bachelor of Education Degree. During the initial job interview, stating I was part of such a history-rich University Hockey Program helped immensely!

In closing...I value education! Education offers opportunity. Opportunity creates destiny. My destiny was to teach Elementary and Junior High School for ten years prior to returning to the University of Alberta to complete a Doctor of Philosophy Degree and teach in the University setting.

I have been recognized an Award-Winning University Teacher Educator and have won National and Provincial Teaching Awards at the Elementary and Junior High School levels as well.

Trust me ... this life path would not have occurred if I never decided to work hard and strive to become part of the CIAU. I was fortunate to earn a Bachelor of Education Degree at one of the most prestigious Universities in the world while being part of one of the most successful University-level Athletics Programs in the nation led by some of the most dedicated, knowledgeable, and talented coaching staffs!

THERE ARE EVEN MORE HOCKEY OPTIONS! If the CIS does not work out for some reason, there are several College Hockey Leagues across Canada (e.g., **Alberta Colleges Athletic Conference - ACAC**).

For goaltenders wishing to extend their hockey careers as they enter their early 20's, College Hockey Leagues offer opportunities to play **competitive hockey** with **high-level coaching** while earning an **education**.

FINANCIAL AID: Besides taking advantage of **education packages** offered by Major Junior "A" Hockey Organizations, there are several Student-Athlete Scholarships that can be earned by goaltenders that choose to join a Canadian University or College Hockey League!

DO YOUR HOMEWORK!

It is up to you to make sure you are aware of all possible Student-Athlete Scholarships available to you!

(e.g., Jimmie Condon Athletic Scholarship).

WEBSITE RESOURCES: The following is merely a brief list to help goaltenders begin to discover the countless opportunities available for them to join a Canadian University or College Hockey Program.

Canadian Inter-University Sport
http://english.cis-sic.ca/landing/index

Alberta Colleges Athletic Conference
http://www.acac.ab.ca/

British Columbia Intercollegiate Hockey League
http://en.wikipedia.org/wiki/British_Columbia_Intercollegiate_Hockey_League

Jimmie Condon Athletic Scholarship
http://alis.alberta.ca/et/fo/scholarships/info.html?EK=30

PART SEVEN

WHAT
ELITE GOALTENDERS
MUST UNDERSTAND

In order for *elite* goaltenders to progress through the hockey ranks, they MUST stay focused on being well-conditioned. Goaltending demands a tonne from specific energy systems. Goaltenders are called upon consistently during hockey games to move quickly for short spurts of time with precision and explosiveness.

ATTENTION PARENTS/GUARDIANS: There are many **Fitness Trainers** and **Conditioning Coaches** in the World of Sports that claim to be knowledgeable enough around the most recent research concerning this topic area. They will sell themselves as the absolute best choice for your goaltender's conditioning needs. Please make sure that what these Trainers and Coaches are claiming can be proven through *proper credentials*, *education,* and *quality experience in the field*.

Please do not fall for the latest unproven, cost-consuming training fad! If you believe there is something strange about a specific training regimen ... *research* it on your own! *DO YOUR HOMEWORK PRIOR TO SPENDING YOUR MONEY!* Trust your instincts when it comes time to choosing your *elite* goaltender's Off-Ice Conditioning Coach.

Once you have selected a quality **Fitness Trainer** or **Conditioning Coach** for your goaltender's off-ice conditioning needs, make sure you are left with some information about how to continue a specific program that can be implemented throughout the hockey season. It is important to allow your goaltender to understand what, when, why, where, and how to train both on-ice and off-ice during the hockey season that will promote safety and success!

IMPORTANT NOTE: It is crucial that goaltenders understand the differences between pre-season, during season, and post-season training. There are different purposes and strategies to gain the most effective use of time when it comes to a goaltender's training regimen in order to become the most conditioned athlete possible.

FOR INSTANCE: Goaltenders can become more conditioned during the off-season by engaging in wind sprint, explosive stair climbing, and roller blading exercises to name a few. In the off-season, it is important to train the muscle groups that are going to be used throughout the hockey season.

CHAPTER 37 - TRAINING CAMPS AND TEAM TRYOUTS

ARE YOU GOING TO BE PREPARED TO PERFORM? This is an extremely important question for goaltenders to ask themselves as training camps draw near. Although the main focus throughout this chapter will be driven toward **elite goaltenders**, all the notes, tips, and ideas should not be overlooked by goaltenders in lower levels of hockey. Goaltenders, at **ALL** levels, should always be identifying strategies that can provide them with an **edge over others** so that they are successful in *training camps* and *team tryouts*.

When goaltenders show up to a training camp, it is imperative that they are prepared both mentally and physically. A training camp MUST not be used to get into shape! Goaltenders that are serious about making a hockey team and impressing the Coaching Staff must be ready to give 100% effort both on and off the ice.

The following is a brief list of some areas that MUST be concentrated on when goaltenders enter training camps. Goaltenders MUST:

1. shake the hands of the Coaching Staff firmly and let them know, in a polite but confident manner, that they are there for one thing, **to make the team**
2. be the first to step onto the ice *ALWAYS*
3. be the last to step off the ice *ALWAYS*
4. be the first to the coach when he/she blows the whistle
5. be the hardest worker, (THE HARDEST WORKER!) on the ice during every single practice, scrimmage, and pre-season game
6. communicate effectively and efficiently both on and off the ice
7. get to know the veteran players and begin the process of developing team spirit in a positive manner
8. be prepared to demonstrate a high level of off-ice conditioning by excelling during all of the physical fitness tests

ATTENTION GOALTENDERS: If you truly want to make a hockey team, get it done! Do not go through the motions and lie to yourself! You will need to become intrinsically motivated because in hockey, there is only one guarantee when it comes to making a hockey team, which is: THERE IS NO GUARANTEE THAT YOU WILL MAKE THE TEAM! In order to make an *elite hockey team*, it will take hours of:

1. training and conditioning (e.g., strength, speed, flexibility, and recovery)
2. practicing goaltender skills (e.g., shuffles, butterfly slides, shooting pucks, hand-eye coordination)
3. dedication to nutrition
4. dedication to proper rest
5. dedication to studying the Game of Hockey

DO YOU HAVE THE EDGE? What makes a Coaching Staff choose one goaltender over another? In other words, during a Junior "A" Hockey Training Camp, it will become very clear that most goaltenders can stop a puck effectively.

What differentiates one goaltender from another goaltender? Some goaltenders will be:

- ✓ older
- ✓ bigger
- ✓ quicker
- ✓ more aggressive
- ✓ more experienced
- ✓ more naturally talented
- ✓ better equipped to play the puck
- ✓ more co-operative amongst team members
- ✓ better equipped to communicate effectively

All Coaching Staffs prepare **Depth Charts** before training camps begin. Prior to training camps, effective Coaching Staffs will have already completed hours and hours of scouting as they attempt to get a good idea of all the talented hockey players (especially goaltenders) that may be invited to their training camps.

The **Depth Chart** is a true assessment guide that assists Coaching Staffs as they strive to solidify their roster. Usually, goaltenders that played on the team during the past season will have their names **pencilled in** as training camp begins.

ATTENTION GOALTENDERS: If you have been one of the goaltenders that played on a particular team last season, it is a *drastic mistake to assume* that your spot on the roster is guaranteed this season! Many goaltenders hit the ice with an attitude of misguided complacency. They believe that they have earned a spot on the team based on their performance from the previous hockey season.

It is certainly true that a goaltender that played exceptionally well last season will be listed at the top of the **Depth Chart** with plenty of patience offered from the Coaching Staff. However, it is extremely IMPORTANT to realize that showing up to training camp in *absolute awful shape* and with a *poor attitude* will quickly force coaches to pull out their erasers in order to make a roster change!

Coach Brent Bradford and Coach Vic LeMire
strongly offer the following advice:

NEVER TAKE ANYTHING FOR GRANTED!!!

IMPORTANT NOTE: The following important advice is pointed toward goaltenders that are striving to make a hockey team for the first time:

Attending Training Camps with an invite NEVER guarantees that you will make the team! In fact, as a new goaltender in the organization, be assured that you will begin with a definite disadvantage that you must overcome in order to be successful.

CAUTION TO PARENTS/GUARDIANS AND GOALTENDERS: It is important for you to be aware and completely knowledgeable about virtually every training camp invite you receive. Many teams simply run several Pre-Training Camps prior to the Main Camp. Certainly, Coaching Staffs monitor each training camp; however, most often they are nothing more than fundraisers for the Hockey Organization!

If you receive an invite to a training camp, it is very important to explore the *true answers* to the following questions:

✓ How many goaltenders will be attending the training camp?
✓ How many goaltenders are **pencilled in** to return to the team from the previous hockey season?

ATTENTION GOALTENDERS: Any training camp that will enrol an extremely high number of goaltenders MUST be avoided completely! There is ONE *sure-fired method* to figure out exactly how sincere the Coaching Staff and/or the Hockey Organization truly feel about YOU!

If the Coaching Staff and/or the Hockey Organization offer you **FREE TUITION** to attend the training camp, this is a good indication that they already know how talented you are and are hoping that you demonstrate all your skills to them!

If you are required to pay for your attendance in a training camp, you must realize immediately that you are on an uphill climb to become part of that **Hockey Team's Depth Chart**.

It is not impossible to make a hockey team from this situation. However, it will take a monumental playing performance on your part to open up the eyes of the Coaching Staff. Your job will be to make it impossible for the Coaching Staff to deny you a spot on the team! Perform so well that the Coaching Staff cannot ignore you!

PREPARE HARD! **WORK HARDER** than every other player on the ice. Use your awesome skills and incredible positive attitude to catch the full attention of the Coaching Staff!

IMPORTANT NOTE: Goaltenders are required to stop pucks; however, if they are **masterful at other dimensions of goaltending** as well, the Coaching Staff will be able to build a team or game plan around them! For instance, a goaltender that can **fire a puck** down the ice productively will be viewed as an asset to a Coaching Staff that enjoys the luxury of having a **third defenseman that hides in the crease** most of the game.

LISTEN UP! A coach can easily tell which goaltenders are listening during a team discussion (e.g., on-ice during practice, in the dressing room prior to or following a practice). Goaltenders are always sending non-verbal messages to potential Coaching Staffs during training camps.

Some **positive non-verbal messages** that goaltenders send are:

➢ showing up at the hockey arena one-hour prior to the on-ice time
➢ being first to step onto the ice
➢ being first to the coach when the whistle blows
➢ being right in front of the coach and kneeling on one knee with an upright posture while the coach is explaining the next drill on the white board
➢ being last to step off the ice

Some *negative non-verbal messages* that goaltenders send are:

- showing up at the hockey arena only minutes prior to the on-ice time
- being *last* to step onto the ice
- being last or in the middle of the pack when skating in when the coach blows the whistle
- kneeling on two knees in the back while the coach is explaining the next drill on the white board
- moving around and/or looking in the stands while the coach is explaining the next drill on the white board
- chatting to others while the coach is talking
- being *first* to step off the ice

ATTENTION GOALTENDERS: Do you see the differences between some of the non-verbal messages that are sent to Coaching Staffs? During your next training camp or team tryout, what messages will you send to your potential Coaching Staff?

IMPORTANT NOTE: Training camps will be a highlight in a goaltender's career. Training camps will be a time when goaltenders reach high levels of success and when they meet many new challenges. Being able to cope with both the successes and the challenges during training camps will be critical for goaltenders if they want to leave a lasting and positive impression on the Coaching Staff!

CHAPTER 38 - A GOALTENDER'S IMAGE

The image a goaltender represents can be just as important as how he/she performs on the ice when it comes to being scouted into *elite* levels of hockey. How a goaltender presents him/herself off the ice sends a clear message to the hockey world. Three very important *image aspects* of becoming an *elite* goaltender are presented below. They are:

1. The Visual Athlete
2. Interviewing Skills
3. Away from the Hockey Arena

1. The Visual Athlete: As a member of a hockey team, you are a very important representative of both your hockey team and your overall hockey community.

Which goaltender would catch your eye first?

ATTENTION GOALTENDERS: The image that you present, both in and around hockey arenas, reflect greatly in the eyes of every hockey scout and hockey coach you meet. Arriving at the hockey arena in a *shirt and tie* prior to a game will send the correct message to scouts and coaches. You will convey a strong personal image, while earning respect from the surrounding people. Looking professional prior to a game will also assist in a strong, confident performance on the ice!

Looking Great = Playing Great!

Once athletes leave the Minor Hockey System to play Junior, University/College or Professional Hockey, it becomes mandatory that they wear a dress shirt, tie, dress pants, and a suit jacket or a stylish team jacket.

Although many Minor Hockey teams fail to request that players should wear a dress shirt and tie to and from the games, every scout will take first notice of you in proper attire, especially if all other players look like they just walked out of an alley!

Do not let other players influence what you wear to games (unless it is a shirt and tie)! The scouts' opinions of you are vastly more important to your hockey future than any player's opinion. Expensive suits are not required! A clean dress shirt and a simple tie will most certainly be a good step forward in your hockey career.

2. Interviewing Skills: As a progressing athlete, *elite* goaltenders will be faced with many interviews and other media contacts. It is important for goaltenders to be aware of this important cog that helps make up the Game of Hockey.

IMPORTANT NOTE: How many times have you watched an athlete make a complete fool of him/herself and/or his/her team, only wishing he/she could take back what was said? It is important to understand that once a goaltender is **on record** with his/her comments, it is done and there is no taking it back.

ATTENTION GOALTENDERS: The athletic media is a very valuable part of sports and, in particular, your hockey career. The media attention may be very beneficial to your hockey career, which might include possible endorsements and even sports media-related jobs once your on-ice career has run its course.

Every aspiring *elite* goaltender must watch, listen, and study regular television interviews that goaltenders and/or players do between periods and during the post-game wrap-ups. It is also important to note that a tremendous amount of learning can occur from watching athletes in other sports interviews as well!

There are several basic interviewing skills that MUST be learned so that you will have less of a chance of **putting your foot into your mouth**! They are as follows:

a) You vs Your Team
b) Your Team vs The Opposition
c) Your Needs vs The Media's Needs
d) Television Interviewing vs Radio Interviewing
e) Remaining Truthful with Your Answers

a) You vs Your Team: Every interviewer will attempt to structure each question by asking about you and your performance in a game. That is totally fair, however, providing your complete thoughts on your own performance will always get back to your teammates, coaching staff, and other teams - guaranteed!

It will be very tempting to let everyone know how great you are, but that is the worst thing that can be verbally communicated. The moment a reporter asks you about something you did, immediately reply by redirecting the question to focus on and complimenting a teammate and/or your team's performance in front of you.

An Example:

Question: *"You made a great save to preserve the shutout tonight! How did you stop that late, third period breakaway?"*

Answer: *"Thank you for that, but, did you notice how hard (teammate's name) back-checked and caused just enough distraction to the shooter so that it made my job easier? Our whole team blocked so many shots for me tonight and cleared the front of the net so effectively that I saw almost every shot! Also, my coaches have spent a great deal of their time working with me and their help has really made the difference!"*

Three things were accomplished with this answer to the reporter's very good question:

✓ the response was directly related to the question
✓ the teammates will appreciate the compliments
✓ the coaches know that you are a good student of the game and are coachable

ATTENTION GOALTENDERS: Your teammates will go through walls for you if they hear you respond to questions like the one stated in the example. Your coaching staff will be comfortable with your progress knowing that they are part of your development.

b) Your Team vs The Opposition: All sorts of interviews will ultimately make their way into the opposition's locker room. They will undoubtedly be posted and highlighted on the **notice boards** to infuriate the players before stepping onto the ice.

It is important to never say a single negative thing about the opposition. As a matter of fact, it is crucial that goaltenders go out of their way to compliment the opposition on several aspects of their team.

c) Your Needs vs The Media's Needs: From time to time, goaltenders may be scheduled or asked to do an interview when they just cannot do it at a specific time. Situations, such as; an injury that requires immediate attention, a family emergency, or a Special Teams meeting that has been called can and should take precedence over an interview.

Of course, informing the media as to the reason why an interview cannot take place is prudent and rescheduling the interview should be decided upon.

IMPORTANT NOTE: The Team Captains usually take the role of co-ordinating interviews for the team. The Captains (in private) should do their best to suggest interviewing players on the team that have not had many opportunities to do interviews in the past.

d) Television Interviews vs Radio Interviews: There is a huge difference between Television and Radio Interviews. The obvious difference is the appearance provided to television watchers and as such, having a simple towel around your neck between periods to wipe your brow is acceptable and appreciated. Showing a classy, proper dress code after the game will cast very positive thoughts of your character without even saying a word.

Although a Radio Interview will not show what you are visually presenting, it will be visible to the radio interviewer. The way he/she perceives you will quite often guide him/her towards the tone of questions asked.

Lastly, a phone interview is the safest interview to provide (visually). However, the questioning must be handled with the same importance and guidelines you would strive to follow from any Television or Radio Interview.

e) Remaining Truthful With Your Answers: Sports interviews become *public entertainment* just like the game. Everything that is stated during an interview can come back to either help your image or hurt your personality badly. Everything that is stated during an interview must be the truth. All interviews are recorded and are subject to review and verification. Goaltenders will never get away with stretching the truth as this will only cause more questions from the media later.

3. Away From The Hockey Arena: You would think that once the game is over and you have gone home or out after the game, you can forget about the image you represent and do whatever you want. The **TRUTH** is that *elite* goaltenders must understand that they are always *under the microscope* with every action and all public conduct will be monitored completely.

The introduction of Facebook, Twitter, and other social network accounts has left each goaltender susceptible to terrible horrors. For example, every Facebook, E-mail, and Twitter comment goaltenders provide **will** become public knowledge and may be open to negative implications.

ATTENTION GOALTENDERS: *NEVER say or print anything you do not want the world to know. Never rely on someone else to keep your comments confidential, as this will NEVER happen!*

LET'S CONCLUDE: Goaltenders, keep your answers short, yet, informative and always complimentary. Give the interviewers what they want, but, do not get caught up with giving out more information than is required. As you listen and begin to study sports interviews, *as we recommend,* you will begin to notice interview answers that become very repetitive in nature.

Elite athletes have learned to prepare basic *stock answers* and they have also learned how to guide the interviewer towards the type of questions they would like to be asked.

Interviewing is both a very important skill that must be learned and an honour should it be requested of you! Always try to bring a positive attitude to the interview with several key points (e.g., teammates, coaches, etc.) that you eventually want to reveal before the interview is over.

Humour and levity will always show confidence in your character and does quite well in an interview. Bring a smile and a laugh to the table as facial features such as smirks or frowns will get you very poor reviews. Of course, *elite* goaltenders **must never** use profanity of any kind as it will reflect on them and their family upbringing and will potentially disgrace them forever! Use polite language during the interview (e.g., speak every word as if it is your Mother and/or Father you are conversing with) and make sure the word *thank you* is stated at the end!

ATTENTION GOALTENDERS: You must learn to become both humble and responsible for your actions every time an interview takes place. Some media personnel enjoy and seek *the dirt* on goaltenders. In some cases, this sells their product and secures their jobs.

A great interviewer will appreciate you as a great interviewee and will conduct the interview quickly with professionalism and consideration of your image. On the contrary, the media will thrive on you if you provide the wrong appearance and provide a very controversial interview as witnessed in the many loud verbal outbreaks observed on TV in the past.

DO NOT become one of those You Tube viral videos!

ATTENTION GOALTENDERS: Demonstrate that you believe you are *blessed* to have been asked for the interview. The media can be your best friend or your worst adversary depending on how you approach them. You must do interviews ... so why not take full advantage of them! With a little practice, you may even begin to enjoy them while becoming a reputable speaker!

PART EIGHT

CONCLUSION

CHAPTER 39 - CONCLUDING THOUGHTS

This book was written to help goaltenders of all ages and ability levels to advance productively through the ranks of hockey. Goaltenders MUST fully understand that it takes an enormous amount of personal effort including; on-ice and off-ice practising, sacrificing social relationships, and maintaining a high level of intrinsic motivation in order to reach the highest levels of hockey. The information explained throughout this book identifies in a clear manner the most important ingredients required to help develop *elite* goaltenders.

We strongly believe that you have gained new insights and effective strategies concerning the **Art of Goaltending** (e.g., on-ice and off-ice information) by reading this book. Now, it is time to begin working toward *elitism*.

REMEMBER THIS POINT GOALTENDERS! No one will hold your hand as you persevere painstakingly through off-season workouts, practice sessions, and video analyses. No one will make sure you did your 5-mile run, 100 shots against the cement wall, push-ups prior to going to sleep, hours of studying video replays (e.g., goaltender saves) shown on TV, etc.! **BUT ... you will know!**

If you cheat yourself, please ask yourself ... **DO YOU REALLY WANT IT!** If the answer is YES ... then go get it ... become an *elite* goaltender and enjoy your journey!

If you reach for the stars and only hit 3/4 of the way ... you are still 3/4 closer toward *elitism* than your buddies who are becoming masters in the latest *online video games* as they sit on their couches all day living sedentary lives!

Who knows ... if you reach 3/4 of the way to the stars, maybe the HOCKEY GODS will reach down 1/4 of the way and lift you up toward the highest levels of hockey!

FINAL WORDS BY
Coach Brent Bradford and Coach Vic LeMire:

If you want it ... begin the process today ... it is waiting for you!

PART NINE

TRIBUTES TO THE GOALTENDER FRATERNITY

A TRIBUTE TO THE MOST SKILLED HOCKEY ANALYSTS
FORMER PROFESSIONAL GOALTENDERS

As you read in this book, many former Professional Goaltenders have transitioned into becoming Hockey Analysts (e.g., radio, internet, television). At the time this book was written, some of the most notable former goaltenders turned Hockey Analysts included: Kelly Hrudey, John Garrett, Darren Pang, Greg Millen, Kevin Weekes, and Jamie McLennan to name a few.

In the next few years, you will undoubtedly see many more former Professional Goaltenders transition into Hockey Analysts. It is not a secret as to why goaltenders make such well-spoken and knowledgeable Hockey Analysts; they understand the Game of Hockey in its entirety.

The reason these former elite goaltenders become such effective game analysts is because they each possess such complete, in depth hockey knowledge which has been garnered from their previous profession. They were fortunate enough to be positioned in the **perfect classroom**; NHL goal nets!

These **Hockey Professors** have been educated in a unique manner by the **University of Hockey.** Each of them has received his Degree by studying the roles, responsibilities, and tendencies of: Coaches, Referees, Forwards, Defensemen, and other Goaltenders in actual game situations under extreme pressures from their very own crease area!

These men **excel** as game analysts because each of them has experience using **vocal instructions** during games as a **General would direct his troops**. They have studied virtually every live game situation scrutinizing each player at both ends of the ice arena making detailed mental notes along the way!

No wonder the pre-game, between period, and post-game analyses shine with such professional expertise!

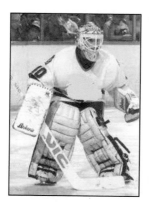 

Thank you Mr. Hrudey, Mr. Garrett, Mr. Pang, Mr. Millen, Mr. Weekes, and Mr. McLennan and all you others who are paving the way for so many goaltenders searching for a **profession after their playing careers wind down**. Also, thank you for sharing your **expertise** and **knowledge** about the **Game of Hockey** and allowing all young, aspiring goaltenders from around the world to learn and analyze what you are stating during your analyses.

While still playing your part in the Goaltender Fraternity ...
You are the True Teachers of the Game!

A TRIBUTE TO THE LEGENDARY SETH MARTIN

I was fortunate to grow up in Trail, BC (aka **The Home of Champions**). I played on many great hockey, baseball, and soccer teams and had terrific teammates. Throughout my childhood, it was drilled in me that two of the greatest feats in sports were when the 1939 (rated the **"Greatest Amateur Team Of All Time"** by **Anatoli Tarasov, Legendary Russian Coach**) and 1961 Trail Smoke Eaters captured the World Hockey Championship Titles. The winning goaltender in 1961 was **Seth 'Cisco' Martin**, who came to be known as **Everybody's All-Star**.

Seth play goal for Team Canada in the World Championships in 1961, 1963, 1964, 1966, and 1967. He was named the Outstanding Goaltender in 1961, 1963, 1964, and 1966 while making the All-World All-Star Team in 1961, 1964, and 1966. He starred for Canada at the Olympics in 1964.

Seth Martin belongs to the: BC Sports, BC Hockey, and IIHF Hall of Fames.

INTERESTING FACTS: Seth Martin, a goaltending pioneer, was the first goaltender to wear a goal mask in International Hockey. In fact, he built many masks for Professional and Amateur Goaltenders, including his NHL goaltender partner Glenn Hall who was wearing one when Bobby Orr scored his famous goal in the 1970 playoffs.

In 1967-1968, Seth played for the NHL's St. Louis Blues. The Blues made it to the Stanley Cup Finals that year. After that season, Seth chose his firefighters pension over an NHL career and returned to Trail, BC where he continued to play and coach hockey.

Seth Martin was nicknamed:
"The Masked Marvel"
by European sportswriters.

DESTINED TO BECOME A GOALTENDER IN TRAIL, BC

Seth Martin is one of the main reasons why I became a goaltender. With such a tremendous goaltender fraternity hailing from Trail, BC (e.g., Seth Martin, Cesare Maniago, Bev Bentley, Don "Smokey" McLeod, Reno Zanier, Mike Zanier), it was apparent to me that small-town goaltenders could reach *elite status* in hockey.

Even in his retirement years, Seth has continued to respect his loyal fans wholeheartedly. He has made himself available to his fans from all over the world; he still signs many autographs and responds to several emails and letters each year. That is what truly makes someone *LEGENDARY!*

A Tribute to Seth Martin:

- *Legendary Goaltender*
- *Professional Athlete*
- *World Champion*
- *3-Time Hall of Famer*

*On December 23, 1964 at Trail's Cominco Arena, the legendary Fred "Cyclone" Taylor presented Seth with the **BCAHA's Outstanding Player Award** as referee Jim Mailey looked on. Seth's WIHL All-Star Team went on to defeat the Russian National Team that night.*

INTERESTING NOTE: *The Great Vladislav Tretiak idolized Seth Martin when he was a young child.*

Thank you Seth for paving the way for so many goaltenders across the world, including myself! Thank you for being open and kind to those who wish to listen to your *rich, descriptive memoirs* and who wish to learn the many lessons you can provide concerning the **Art of Goaltending**!

ATTENTION GOALTENDERS: When you are studying the history of goaltenders … be sure to look up Seth Martin. He truly made a positive impact in what we all belong to … **THE GOALTENDER FRATERNITY!**

/Brent Bradford

A TRIBUTE TO THE MEN IN THE NETS

ATTENTION YOUNG 6 - 12 YEAR OLD GOALTENDERS: How awesome it is to go to bed at night after watching another great National Hockey League game with your family; one in which your favourite goaltender was named the **STAR OF THE GAME** once again?

TIME TO DREAM: With your bedroom walls plastered with your favourite goaltender posters and all those many special hockey figurines and player cards lining the top of your desk, lay your head down onto your pillow in a darkened room and, with your eyes closed, dream and imagine yourself becoming **"the Man in the Net"** making all those great, game-winning saves for your team.

Crozier Recognized by the NHL!

*In 2000, the NHL unveiled the **Roger Crozier Award** for the goaltender with the highest saves % in each regular season.*

Whether it is 1951 or 2011, for every aspiring young goaltender, the DREAM is the same! The DREAM of becoming the next legendary and all-inspiring goaltender has remained constant throughout time!

Roger Crozier played 518 regular season games in the NHL. He earned 206 wins and 30 shutouts. He had a career GAA of 3.04 and suited up for Detroit, Buffalo, Washington.

His big-league debut was in 1963 as a 21 year old call-up from the AHL Pittsburgh Hornets.

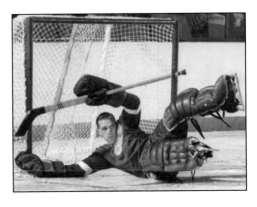

Crozier was absolutely amazing in the nets! */Vic LeMire*

THANK YOU TO THE ORIGINAL LEGENDS OF THE GAME!

- **Roger Crozier** and **Terry Sawchuck** and **Clint Benedict**
- **Glenn Hall** and **Jaques Plante** and **Cecil Thompson**
- **Gump Worsley** and **Johnny Bower** and **Georges Vezina**
- **Emile Francis** and **George Hainsworth** and **Turk Broda**
- **Alec Connell** and **Bill Durnan** … the list continues …

Even throughout our life-time, we have been blessed to watch, with our very own eyes, *elite goaltenders* becoming future legends!

THANK YOU TO THE FUTURE LEGENDS OF THE GAME!

- **Ken Dryden** and **Cesare Maniago** and **Tony Esposito**
- **Olaf Kolzig** and **Grant Fuhr** and **Mike Richter**
- **Martin Brodeur** and **Patrick Roy** and **Richard Brodeur**
- **Kelly Hrudey** and **Ed Belfour** and **Bernie Parent**
- **Pete Peeters** and **Tim Thomas** and **Roberto Luongo**
- **Bill Ranford** and **Ron Hextall** … the list continues …

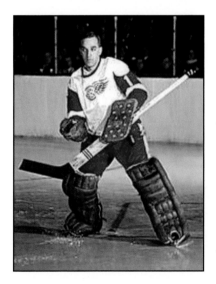

Roger Crozier was identified as an elite goaltender at an early age. At age 14, he became the starting goaltender for his hometown's senior hockey team. He spent his Junior Hockey career playing for the St. Catherine's Teepees of the Ontario Hockey Association from 1959 to 1962.

In 1964-1965, Crozier started all 70 games for the Red Wings (his first full year). He led the league with 40 wins and 6 shutouts.

ATTENTION GOALTENDERS: Although the game has changed and will continue to throughout time, it is **"the Men in the Nets"**, (the LEGENDS throughout time) who make our dreams come true! Always remember that we are all part of … **THE GOALTENDER FRATERNITY**!

Thank you Roger Crozier … for INSPIRING me! /Vic LeMire

PICTURE SOURCES

Below is a list of information regarding the sources for the pictures that were selected for *Goaltenders are not Targets*:

Ball Peen Hammer (Page 20)
http://ssl.gstatic.com/gb/images/b_8d5afc09.png

Marc-Andre Fleury (Page 24)
http://www.google.ca/search?q=marc+andre+fleury&hl=en&client=firefox-a&hs=Cn2&rls=org.mozilla:enUS:official&prmd=imvnso&tbm=isch&tbo=u&source=univ&sa=X&ei=mSaBTtzHGsjniALJ44X4DA&ved=0CEQQsAQ&biw=1440&bih=781

Tim Thomas (Page 61)
http://www.google.ca/search?q=tim+thomas+montreal+pictures&hl=en&client=firefoxa&hs=UKi&rls=org.mozilla:enUS:official&prmd=imvnso&tbm=isch&tbo=u&source=univ&sa=X&ei=pimBTseCFubiiALerPz7DA&ved=0CCUQsAQ&biw=1440&bih=781

Gump Worsley (Page 83)
http://t0.gstatic.com/images?q=tbn:ANd9GcSnUmmLq2gkUZlrXOZrLqbY_jaribtDPa3fkBF_bVWHJyOfHThRw

Jacques Plante (Page 83)
http://t1.gstatic.com/images?q=tbn:ANd9GcTg0mQCOx5Hm1V8wdKd9b7sPfPu027culUIfAeqvsJGVh8ngncLeg

Roberto Luongo (Page 84)
http://t2.gstatic.com/images?q=tbn:ANd9GcQhceHw1Ak3HyQGmk7vz9iNoeJwFFWUsM1SLw3gKqWz4seywGg1uQ

Miikka Kiprusoff (Page 84)
http://t0.gstatic.com/images?q=tbn:ANd9GcQ5_ckwVuStf9Em545QdaQxE2A9i7Xo74Jn_lHjampJ18PR8so3EA

Marty Turco (Page 85, 156)
http://sharkspage.com/galleries/2006_sharks_dallas1/images/sharks_dallas9.jpg

Kelly Hrudey (Page 215)
http://www.goaliestore.com/board/Classifieds/data/32/KGrHqUOKiEE30O70qqIBOKPpkD6R_12.jpg

Kelly Hrudey (Page 215)
http://helpinghanddsrf.org/helpinghand/_view/layouts/images_handprints/hs_14335.jpg

John Garrett (Page 216)
http://www.hockeygoalies.org/trivia/pictures/year13week15.jpg

John Garrett (Page 216)
http://t1.gstatic.com/images?q=tbn:ANd9GcTamTTv8mwSjJ_Yb7C1ZOhxDuyqlBIax_y_El8rSeExpNExHDT8

| Darren Pang | (Page 216) |
| | http://t0.gstatic.com/images?q=tbn:ANd9GcR7KCSrHenR6v1VSLY0DieH4s-B9MUEr8eCBbJ-98CGOhZzL_qp |

| Darren Pang | (Page 216) |
| | http://t2.gstatic.com/images?q=tbn:ANd9GcTgsK4d3Rv6qRn7rnKyH7waHoL5CvdlbiTRQl87jUWaQq4duEssOgSPkmCj |

| Seth Martin | (Pages 217, 218) |
| | http://www.google.ca/search?q=seth+martin&hl=en&client=firefox-a&hs=5Q2&rls=org.mozilla:en-US:official&prmd=imvnso&tbm=isch&tbo=u&source=univ&sa=X&ei=PiGBTo2sEoTQiAKg6_2ADQ&ved=0CDkQsAQ&biw=1440&bih=781 |

| Roger Crozier | (Page 84, 219) |
| | http://img.fanbase.com/media.fanbase.com/8/38072/0653c4b1069d880bfc718abdc22dc5b01ed4a053.jpg?x=450&y=360&sig=c96dfb374bc747649e8719acc73c0309 |

| Roger Crozier | (Page 219) |
| | http://blog.detroitathletic.com/wp-content/uploads/2010/04/Roger-Crozier.jpg |

| Roger Crozier | (Page 220) |
| | http://www.google.ca/imgres?imgurl=http://www.sabreslegends.com/crozier_r_det.jpg&imgrefurl=http://www.sabreslegends.com/crozier_r_bio.html&h=300&w=232&sz=16&tbnid=mqBvZn_bjrgFpM:&tbnh=91&tbnw=70&prev=/search%3Fq%3Droger%2Bcrozier%26tbm%3Disch%26tbo%3Du&zoom=1&q=roger+crozier&docid=qSSNFBGclyyjgM&sa=X&ei=UiOBTrj7A67YiAKQ8IiiDQ&ved=0CDwQ9QEwBA&dur=519 |

Special thanks to the following people for their contributions with pictures:

➢ *Brent Bradford*
➢ *Victor LeMire*
➢ *Kodi Couture*
➢ *Biagio Veltri*
➢ *Bradford's Goal Academy*
➢ *Langley Thunder Hockey Team 2010/11*
➢ *Powell River Paper Kings Hockey Team 2010/11*
➢ *BCHL*

Brent Bradford, M.Ed. & Vic LeMire

Are you tired of everyone borrowing *"Your"* copy of the book?

Simply send them to our Website

<u>GoaliesAreNotTargets.com</u>

They can purchase their copies in either our
Soft Cover Book **or our** E-Book **format!**